Editions of this book will appear simultaneously in France, Great Britain, Italy and the Netherlands under the auspices of Euredition bv, Den Haag, Netherlands

This edition published by Magna Books, Magna Road, Wigston, Leicester LE18 4ZH, England

ISBN 1 85422 863 3

Translation: Tony Langham
Typesetting: Zspiegel grafische zetterij, Best

Printed in The Netherlands by Royal Smeets Offset, Weert

Production: VBI/SMEETS
Compilation: BoekBeeld, Utrecht
Design and text of plan, planting plan, flowering and colour scheme: Bureau Willemien Dijkshoorn BNT, Amsterdam
Editor A-Z: Yvonne Taverne, Utrecht
Editor-in-chief: Suzette E. Stumpel-Rienks, Bennekom
Photographs: Plant Pictures World Wide, Haarlem
Planning and maintenance, text: Suzette E. Stumpel-Rienks, Bennekom;
Drawings: Theo Schildkamp, Haaksbergen
Small workers in the garden, text and drawings: Theo Schildkamp, Haaksbergen

Borders

Flowers & Plants

MAGNA BOOKS

Contents

Index

Introduction

A lavish garden

The subject of this attractive book deals is stocking your borders with perennials. In many gardens they make up the most colourful part of the planting scheme and a lavish garden is almost unimaginable without these plants. Borders skilfully arranged with perennials is visually satisfactory because of the variation and composition. There are a great many different perennials available, not only in terms of varieties, but also in terms of colour and height, from low creepers to plants reaching more than 2 m in height. We have narrowed down this large selection to one that is manageable - with extensive detail and beautifully illustrated in the book's A-Z section.
More than 30 species are used to achieve the design and also as ground cover. Height, flowering seasons and cultivation have all been taken into account, so that for a large part of the year a harmonious interplay between shape and form can be enjoyed.
Many perennials are herbaceous, a number of species dying back to ground level during the winter and hibernating underground, only to come up again in the spring. Many are evergreen and create an attractive effect in the garden in winter. After three years the garden will have matured and maintenance has to be dealt with. To maintain the harmonious balance, fast spreading plants will need to be kept in check to protect their more timid neighbours.
The aim of this book is primarily to give useful hints for pleasing results, or simply to enjoy your plants more.

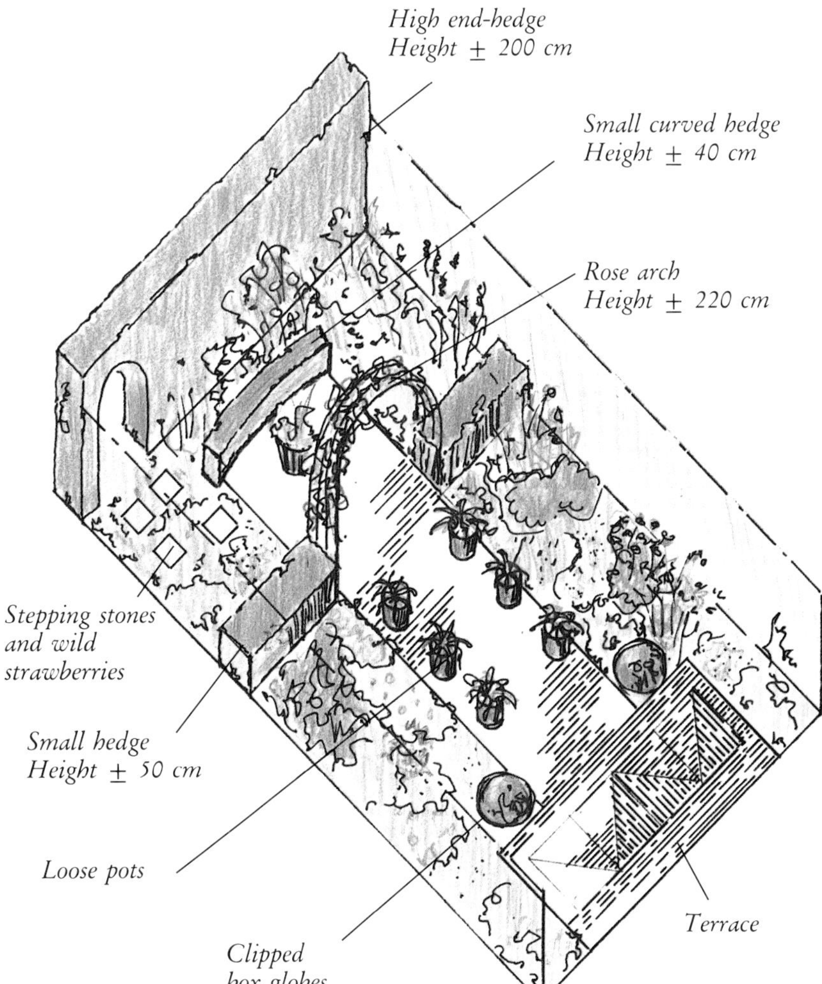

Bird's-eye-view drawing.
A fallow piece of land, dug over and improved with the right additives and planted up according to the plan. After 2 - 3 years the garden reaches its full glory. All being well, the garden will look something like this.

Design

The point of departure for the design of this garden is a symmetrical layout of the available space. The use of perspective makes the garden appear deeper and bigger. The basic elements to be included in the design are as follows:
- a terrace, with space for a table and chairs;
- a long (brick) paved path, closed off by a hedge which is slightly curved;
- two-thirds of the way down the garden two small clipped square hedges and a rose arch;
- this arrangement makes the distance to the end-hedge appear greater;
- the box globes and the loose pots on the path emphasize the three-dimensional effect.

The pots can be placed on the terrace or temporarily amongst the plants in the border.

Above:
This design emphasizes the width of the surface. Once the rather intensive planting is completed, little maintenance will be necessary. The layout is relatively 'durable' and provides a play area for children. This design is developed further in another booklet in this series.

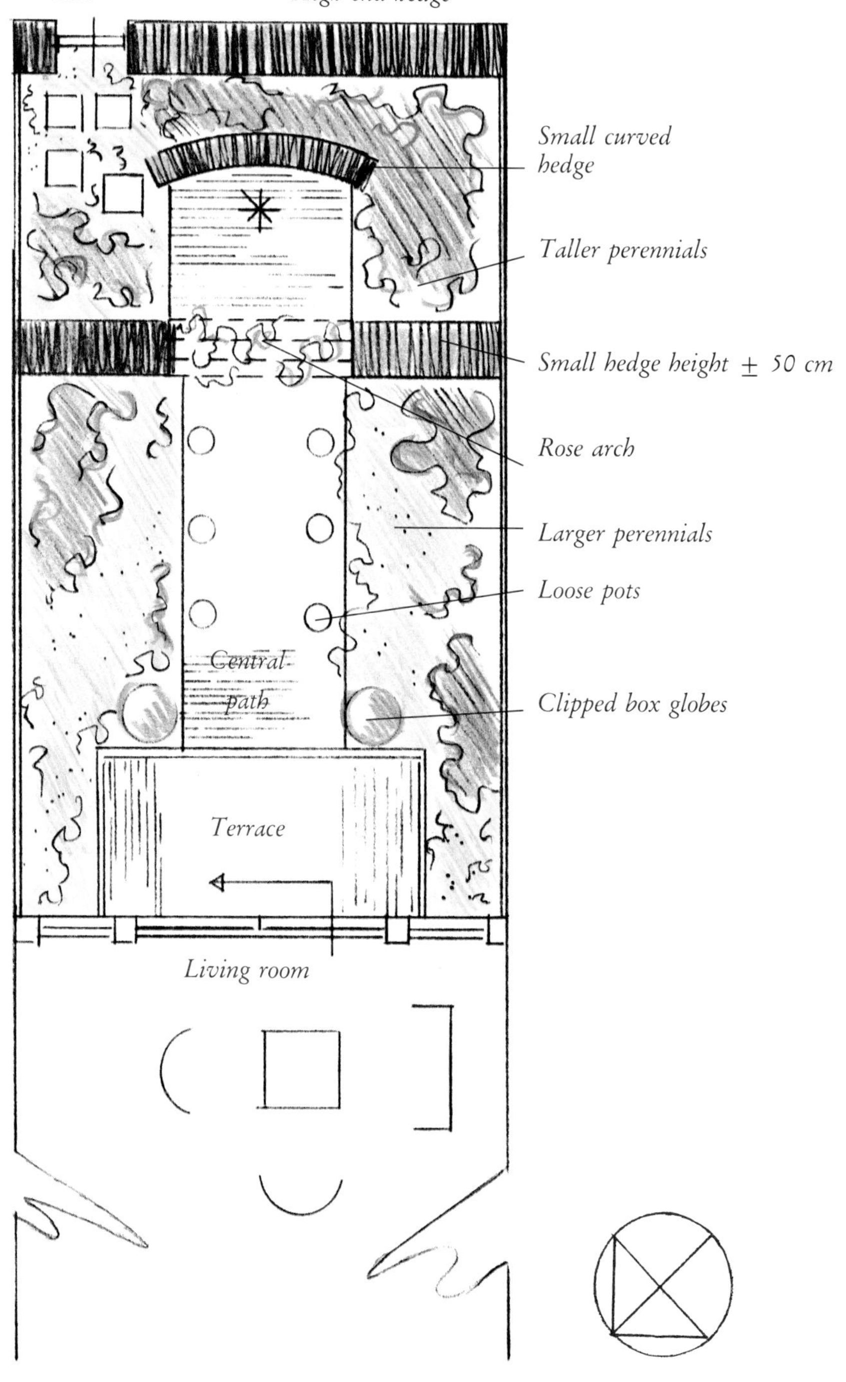

Below:
The diagonally-placed stepping stones leading to a shady pergola increase the feeling of depth. With the exception of the terrace, which acts as a break in the design, the space is completely taken over by the planting scheme, which can create a magical oasis of flowers.

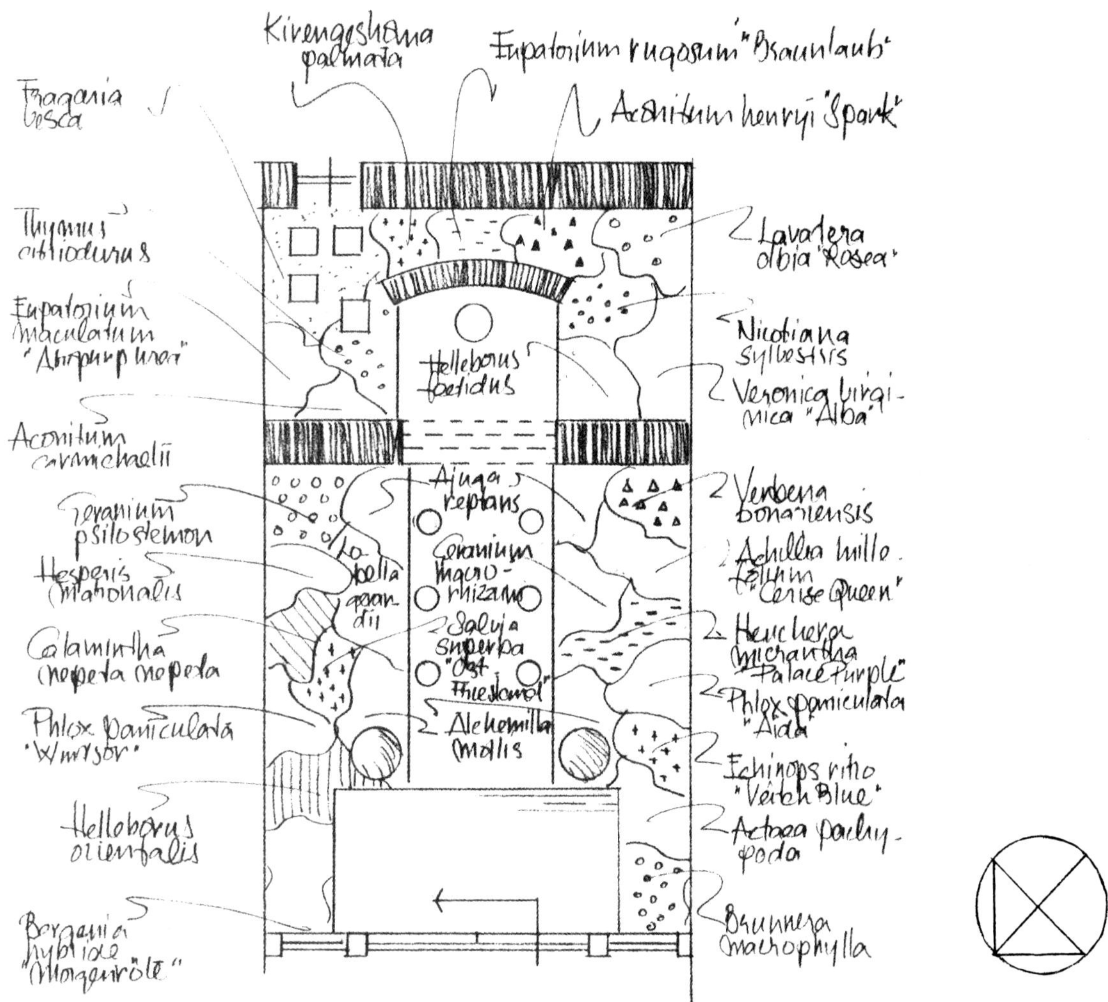

Planting scheme

The idea behind the planting scheme is to create an interesting mixture of growth patterns, foliage and flowering shapes in combined groups. In a well-manured and a well turned-over soil a lushly flowering area will take shape as early as the first year. Once the terrace and path have been laid, the first hedges are put in, after which the plants are bedded in the marked spots, including at least 5 to 6 of each desired variety. Water well. After this, the plants will fend for themselves, grow and flower. This garden will have to be re-arranged every 4 to 5 years.

The figures indicate the various flowering times: the early flowering varieties are placed near the wall so that they can be enjoyed from the house early in the year.

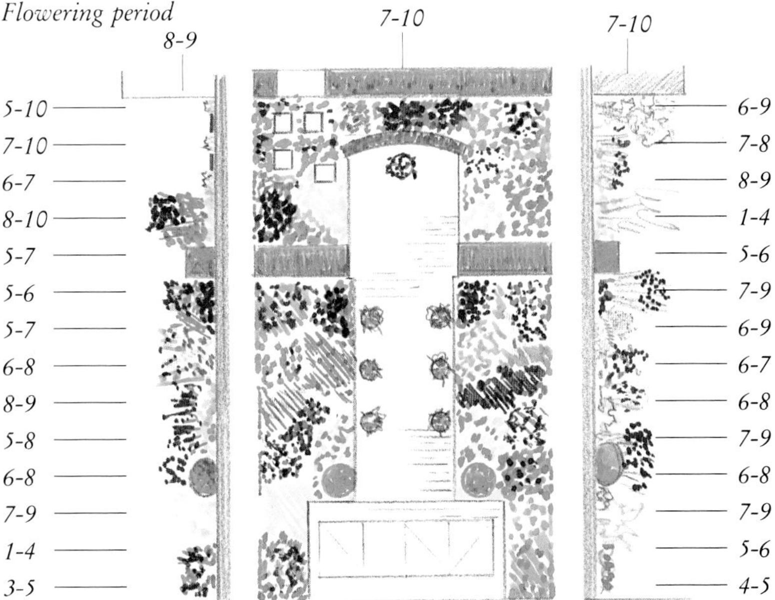

Acanthus mollis

Acanthus

○ ↕ 80-100 ○ ❁ 7-8 ✂

Both the beautiful, deeply indented leaves and the sturdy stems with their striking, bristly, serrated, deep purple veined bracts of *Acanthus* (from the Greek word "akantha" = spine) are very attractive. In architecture these leaves were used to decorate the capitals of Corinthian pillars with the well-known "acanthus motif". The stalkless, deeply indented leaves of *A. mollis*, which originates in Mediterranean regions, are covered with soft hairs and have a shiny, dark green colour. The flowering ears have greenish-purple bracts and purplish-white flowers. *A. mollis* "Latifolius" can grow to a height of 1.5 m. *A. spinosus* has pinkish-violet flowers and dark green leaves with large spines. This is a good plant to grow in isolation (approximately 3 plants per m^2); it needs light, nutritious soil, which is not too moist. In severe frost, cover with straw. For cut flowers, wait until the cluster of flowers has completely developed, and remove a lot of the foliage to prevent evaporation. Propagate from seed and root cuttings. Attracts bees.

Achillea

Yarrow

○ ↕ 30-60 ○ ❁ 7-9 ✻ ✂

It is said that the Greek hero, Achilles, who inspired the name of this genus, was quickly cured from the injuries he sustained in war, by the use of the leaves of *A. millefolium* on his wounds.
Achillea is found in the northern hemisphere. *A. millefolium*, indigenous yarrow, is common along road verges, on dykes, and in barren grassland. It has finely segmented leaves, and flowers with white or pale pink florets which form a sort of umbel. There are many extremely hardy cultivated varieties in pinks and reds. *A. millefolium*, "Cerise Queen", has cherry-red flowers; "Red Beauty" has dark red flowers; "Christel" has bright red flowers; "Lilac Beauty" has lilac flowers, and *Achillea* "Schwefelblüte" has pale yellow flowers. Like the original species, they are good cut flowers. This plant has few special requirements, and tends to grow rather wild, so that it is suitable for gardens of wild flowers. The stalks should be cut at ground level when the plants have flowered. Propagate from seed or divide plants. Attracts flies.

Aconitum carmichaelli "Arendsii", Monkshood

Achillea millefolium "Christel", Yarrow

Aconitum

Monkshood

50-150 7-9 !

The name of this plant is derived from the Greek word, "akoniton", which was the name of a plant to poison wolves and other predators. It indicates that the plant is poisonous ! It is indigenous in central and southern Europe, and has strikingly shaped blue or bright purple or (occasionally) yellow flowers, which flower in remarkably long clusters. The upper petal is reminiscent of a helmet or monk's hood. The shining dark green leaves are deeply indented and palmate. *A. carmichaelii* has leathery leaves and bluish-violet flowers. *A. carmichaelii* "Arendsii" has large dark-blue flowers on stiff stems which stand erect. *A. henryi* "Spark" (syn. "Spark's Variety") has large, purplish-blue flowers and is excellent for cut flowers. *A. pyrenaicum* has yellow flowers. Good garden soil (not a heavy clay soil), rich in humus, moist, cool, slightly shaded. After flowering, cut back the stalks. For cut flowers, the first buds must be open. Propagate from seed and by dividing the plant.
Attracts bumble bees.

Actaea

Doll's eyes, White baneberry

30-80 7-8 !

The Greek demigod, Actaeon, was well aware that the berries of this plant are poisonous. To punish him for spying on Artemis and her nymphs as they were bathing, the goddess turned him into a deer and he was then devoured by his own dogs, who had been maddened by eating the berries of the plant which was subsequently named after him.

Actaea is indigenous in temperate woodland regions in the northern hemisphere. It has luxuriant, double, triple or multiple divided leaves with a serrated edge. In May/June, clusters of small, white flowers appear on fairly tall stems. They look rather fluffy because of their protruding stamens. However, the decorative aspect of this plants is determined by the berries, which can be white, red or black, depending on the species. *A. pachypoda* (syn: *A. alba*) has white berries which grow on thick, stiff, reddish stems; *A. rubra* has red berries on thin stems; *A. spicata* is a black poisonous berry.

Moist soil, rich in humus, cool. Propagate from seed and by dividing the plant. Attracts insects which collect pollen.

Actaea pachypoda, White baneberry

Ajuga reptans "Burgundy Glow"

Ajuga

15-25  5-6

Creeping ajuga, *A. reptans*, is fairly common throughout Europe in moist, shady spots. This low-growing plant makes excellent ground cover.

The erect, flowering stem with attractive clusters of blue (or occasionally pink or white) clusters of flowers protrudes above the leaves from a rosette of dark green, spatulate leaves. The plant can spread rapidly - though it does not run riot - by sending runners from the rosette which creep along the ground, take root, and then form new rosettes. *A. reptans* "Atropurpurea" grows less rapidly, and has purplish, bronze- coloured leaves. *A. reptans* "Variegata" has greyish-green leaves with cream-coloured spots and a cream edge; *A. reptans* "Burgundy Glow" has bronze-green leaves with a cream edge. *A. reptans* "Purple Torch" has purple flowers.

Moist, well-drained soil. Cultivated varieties with colourful leaves should be placed in a sunny spot. Propagate by dividing plant or by removing runners which have taken root; plant in moist soil.

Alcea
Hollyhock

• •• ↕ 150-300 ↔ 30-50 ○ 7-9 ✂

Although *Alcea* (sometimes erroneously referred to as *Althaea*) is a perennial plant in Asia Minor, it is often cultivated as an annual or biennial. The leafy, flowering ear, which has short-stemmed, bell-shaped flowers at the top, singly or in groups in the leaf axilla, develop from a rosette consisting of leaves with five to seven lobes. There are many colours: red, pink, violet, deep purple, purple, yellow, white, and all sorts of shades in between. There are also varieties with stripes, flames and spots. The flowers of cultivated varieties vary enormously in colour and shape, and have a diameter of 10 cm or more. They can be single, double or (semi) composite.
A. rosea "Nigra", the black hollyhock, is a biennial plant and has single, very deep purple flowers. *A. rosea* "Annua", the summer hollyhock, is an annual, and grows to 1-1.5 m. It has single flowers, one colour or mixed. *A. rosea* "Chater's Double" is a biennial, 1.75-2 m, with large, composite flowers in many colours, up to 15 cm in diameter. "Icicle" has white flowers and "Newport Pink" has pale pink flowers. It requires a lot of space, moist and well-drained soil, which is not too wet in winter. Protect from the wind, e.g., by planting against a wall. Sensitive to rust. Reject affected flowers. Propagate from seed and cuttings.

Alcea rosea, hybrid, Hollyhock

Alchemilla mollis "Robustica", Ladies' mantle

Anaphalis
Pearl everlasting

20-30 10-30 7-8

With its silvery-grey leaves and white flowers, *Anaphalis* is suitable for combining with other plants in borders, and is sufficiently sturdy to serve as support for taller, less sturdy perennials growing next to it. The flowers have the characteristic appearance of straw flowers, and are often used in bouquets of dried flowers.
A. triplinervis originates from the Himalayas. It has narrow, silver-coloured leaves with three clear veins. The bottom of the leaves is covered with white, woolly hair. The silvery-white flowers grow in small clusters. *A. triplinervis* "Sommerschnee" grows to a height of 50 cm, and has bright, white flowers.
A. margaritacea is less tall, and has pearly-white flowers and greyish-green, hairy, woolly leaves. It is very suitable as a supporting plant.
This plant requires dry or not too moist soil, preferably chalky. For dried flowers, the flowers must be picked before they have opened completely, and must be placed in the shade to dry. Propagate by cutting rootstocks in the dormant period (October to March), and seed in a cold frame (March-April), or outside (mid-April).

Alchemilla
Ladies' mantle

30-50 35-40 5-8

Alchemilla is found in many parts of Europe and Asia. The round indented leaves are a yellowish or bluish green, and hairy to a greater or lesser extent. The yellow flowers grow in loose plumes.
A. xanthochlora is indigenous in western Europe and can be found in grasslands, on the edges of woods, and along verges and ditches. It has a few hairy leaves, and greenish-yellow plumes. *A. mollis* has hairy, fan-shaped leaves, and soft, light, yellowish-green plumes. *A. mollis* "Robustica" is larger, and suitable for cut flowers.
Any sufficiently moist garden soil is suitable; support with canes or using adjacent plants. Preferably plant in spring. The flowers are often used in bouquets of dried flowers. Propagate by dividing the plants. In moist soil, rich in humus, *Alchemilla* will self-seed profusely; the plant also thrives in gardens of wild flowers.

Anchusa
Ox-tongue

60-150 30 4-8

The name *Anchusa* (from the Greek word "anchusa", which means red) refers to the red dye obtained from the roots, which was used for make-up in the past. The plant owes its English name, "Ox-tongue", to its rough, hairy leaves. The blue flowers are very similar to those of forget-me-nots.
The genus is indigenous in Europe, northern and southern Africa and western Asia, and comprises both annual and perennial varieties.
A. officinalis, wild ox-tongue, is sometimes found along sandy roads or in dunes.
The hairy, narrow, greyish-green leaves are

Anaphalis triplinervis, Pearl everlasting

Anchusa azurea, Ox-tongue

erect; the purplish-blue flowers grow on stems in the leaf axilla. *A. italica* (syn. *A. azurea*) has very hairy, lanceolate, green leaves, and flowers profusely with clusters of blue flowers. The plant branches out, and grows to a height of 1.5 m. It may have to be tied to prevent it from collapsing. *A. italica* "Little John" has bright blue flowers, and grows to a height of only 60 cm; "Loddon" has large, gentian blue flowers; "Dropmore" is taller and has small, dark blue flowers.
It does best in fertile, well-drained soil, too dry rather than too wet; protect in winter by covering. Propagate from root cuttings and seed.
Attracts bees.

Aquilegia "William Guinness", Columbine

Aquilegia
Columbine

40-80 5-6

These elegant plants, which are found in Europe and North America, have strikingly attractive flowers with long spurs. The varieties with composite flowers are a plus point in any garden and make excellent cut flowers.
A. vulgaris, the common columbine, has beautiful, large, hanging, blue or dark purple flowers. It also grows in the wild and can proliferate. *A. vulgaris* "Nivea" has large white flowers; "Nora Barlow" has composite, pinkish-white flowers.
A. chrysantha has golden-yellow flowers and long spurs. Together with *A. caerulea*, which has blue flowers, it has produced many hybrids. "Crimson Star" is crimson with a yellowish-white heart; "Mrs. Kana's Giants" has large flowers in many pastel shades; "Mrs. Scott-Elliot" is bluish, crimson or white.
It requires normal, moist garden soil, rich in humus, well-drained. *A. vulgaris* does best in semi-shaded, slightly chalky soil, not too moist in winter, cover with straw. Propagate from seed (autumn) and by diving the plant (spring).
The spurs contain a lot of nectar which can only be reached by bumble bees with very long probosci. Other visitors (such as honeybees, simply bore a hole into the spur (breaking and entering).

Arabis

10-30 4-6

The white (composite) flowers of *A. caucasica* and its varieties blossom profusely. The plant is indigenous in the northern hemisphere. It forms rosettes of grey leaves with lilac or white flowers. It is an evergreen, and will grow easily in any open place.
A. caucasica grows wild in western Europe. With its greyish-green, white leaves and luxuriant white flowers, it tends to sprawl, but it is an excellent border plant.
A. caucasica "Plena" has composite white flowers; "Schneehaube" is good for cut flowers and grows in a fairly compact way; "Hedi" has deep pink flowers. *A. x arendsii*

has pink flowers and a rather stunted growth. *A. procurrens* has smooth green leaves and white flowers and makes excellent ground cover.
Normal garden soil, slightly sandy. Removing the stems after the plant has flowered encourages it to flower again (less profusely).
Propagate from seed and by dividing the plant.

Artemisia

○ ↕ 15-180 ○ ✿ 7-9

Artemisia is common in the northern hemisphere. It comprises a number of interesting herbs, such as lad's love, tarragon and absinthe. The plant derives its decorative value from its attractive grey leaves; the flowers are less attractive.
A. absinthium "Lambrook Silver" has beautiful grey leaves. It is a hardy plant and grows to a height of 80 cm. *A. lactiflora* grows up to 180 cm tall. It has pronounced, pinnate feathered leaves which are 20 cm long and dark green on the upper surface, and milky white, fragrant flowers (September/October). It is susceptible to fungi. *A. ludoviciana*, up to 100 cm tall, has attractive grey, felt-like aromatic leaves, and yellow flowers from July to September.
A. ludoviciana "Silver Queen", 70-90 cm, has grey leaves. *A. schmidtiana* "Nana" is less than 30 cm tall. It has silvery-grey leaves and attractive white flowers in June/July; it is moderately hardy in winter.
A. stelleriana, 30-60 cm tall, forms a splendid carpet with its grey stems and creeping growth. It requires slightly drier soil, and is moderately hardy in winter.
In general, it requires good, porous garden soil. Propagate by dividing the plant and plant immediately.

Artemisia ludoviciana, Alsem, and Campanula lactiflora "Loddon Anna"

Arabis caucasica "Hedi"

Aruncus

Goat's beard

 150-200 6-7

The growth of *A. dioicus* (syn. *A. sylvestris*), European goat's beard is rather slow in the first few years, but becomes increasingly profuse with cream-coloured plumes which are in fact quite reminiscent of a goat's beard.
The beautiful big leaves on long stems are bipinnate or tripinnate and grow in threes, with serrated edges. There are male and female plants. The female plumes are yellowish-white, the male plumes appear later, and are bright white and have a more elegant shape. *A. dioicus* "Kneiffii" has slightly narrower, more pointed leaves, and grows to a height of 60 cm.
The plant requires a clay soil, rich in humus, not too dry. Other soil needs manure and some lime. For propagating from seed, there must be both male and female plants. Flies will fertilize the female flowers. Young plants can easily be dug up and transplanted. It is also possible to divide the plants (March/April, or in October).

Aster alpinus "Albus"

Aruncus dioicus, Goat's beard

Aster

15-250 20-25 5-7-11

Most *Aster* varieties which grow naturally are found in North America and China; only a few are indigenous in Europe and South Africa. However, there are many varieties available which are subdivided according to when they flower; spring asters, which have one flower on each stem, and summer and autumn asters which branch out, and often have hairy stems. The height and colour of asters are very variable; the daisy-like flowers often have a yellow heart.
Spring asters include *A. alpellus* "Triumph", 15 cm, June/July, violet with an orange heart; *A. alpinus*, 15-25 cm, May/June, lilac. *A. alpinus* "Alba", 30 cm, white; *A. tongolensis* "Wartburgstern", 30-40 cm, May/June, deep purple, summer/autumn asters: *A. amellus*, 80 cm, July to September, lilac; *A. dumosus* hybrids, 15-40 cm, August to October, all sorts of shades of blue, pink

and white. *A. ericoides*, 80-100 cm, September to October, white or pink; *A. novae-angliae*, 60-250 cm, September to October, pink, blue and lilac; *A. novi-belgii*, 80-150 cm, September to November, white, purple, red, lilac. There are many cultivated varieties of all the above in every shade of blue, purple, pink, red and white.
Any loose, moist, but not too wet garden soil is suitable, preferably lime-rich. Remove stems when the plants have flowered. Propagate by dividing plants; in older plants, the outer parts of the clump. Susceptible to mildew; discard (burn) affected plants.

Astilbe

Spirea

40-120 6-8

When the leaves of *Astilbe* curl, it is a sign that the soil is too dry. This plant, which originates from Japan, requires moist soil. The serrated leaves grow in double sets of three, and have a coppery or bronze sheen during the summer months. The plumes can be broad or slender, and exist in shades of red, pink, purple, white and lilac.
A. x arendsii has long waving plumes in white, pink or red, and many hybrids are often seen in borders or by ponds. "Bressingham Beauty" grows to a height of 150 cm and has pink plumes; "Cattleya", 100 cm, has pink plumes; "Fanal", 60-100 cm, is purplish-red with brownish-red leaves; "Irrlicht", is white. *A. chinensis* "Pumila", the only variety which tolerates slightly drier soil, grows to a height of 30 cm. It is a creeper with small pink, flowering plumes from July to September.
Any moist, nutritious soil is suitable; add compost in April; protect by covering in winter. Cut stems when the plant has finished flowering. Propagate by dividing the plant (in spring).

Astilbe x arendsii "Cattleya", Spirea

Astrantia major "Rosensymphonie", Masterwort

Bergenia

30-50 4-5

In the past the roots of *B. crassifolia* were used as a lye to prepare leather for making shoes. This variety is rarely cultivated nowadays.
Bergenia is an evergreen plant from Mongolia, Siberia and Afghanistan. It has leathery leaves which turn from green to brown in autumn and winter. A thick, bare reddish stem with white, pale or dark pink clusters of flowers develops in the centre of the rosette of leaves. They are about 30 cm long. The almost round, shiny leaves often remain attractive in winter.
B. cordifolia has pale lilac or dark pink flowers; *B. pupurascens* is purplish-red; *Bergenia* "Abendglut" is dark red with dark leaves; "Morgenröte" is pink to purplish-red; "Silberlicht" is white.

Astrantia

Masterwort

50-70 6-8

The inflorescence of this ornamental plant from central and southern Europe looks rather like a knot. The white or red involucre leaves are larger than the pink flowers, which grow on stems in umbels. The palmate, shiny green leaves on the rather bare stems have five indentations and a serrated edge.
A. major has pink or greenish flowers; *A. major* "Rosea" and "Rosensymphonie" have a red inflorescence; "Rubra" blossoms with pinky-red flowers. *A. maxima* is not as tall (50 cm) and has leaves with three indentations and large, light pink involucre leaves.
The plant prefers moist, fertile, light clay soil. Protect from bright sunshine. Propagate by dividing the plant (in spring).

This plant is easy to grow; it requires normal moist soil, and a sheltered spot, not too warm. Propagate by dividing the rootstock. It takes a long time before the plant flowers if it is grown from seed.

Bergenia cordifolia hybrid

Brunnera macrophylla, Caucasian forget-me-not

Brunnera

Caucasian forget-me-not

○ ↕ 40-60 ◐ ❀ 4-5 ❄

This plant, which originates from the Caucasus, has blue flowers, rather like forget-me-nots, in loose plumes, early in the year (April). The attractive, heart-shaped, hairy leaves on the thin flower stems do not have any stalks and develop when the plant has almost finished flowering, but then they remain attractive all through the summer. The single leaves have a long stalk. *B. macrophylla* tolerates semi-shaded and shaded spots, and is also suitable for planting under shrubs. *B. macrophylla* "Variegata" has coloured leaves and requires more light for the leaves to come into their own. The plant prefers moist soil, rich in humus. In winter it is sensitive to standing water. Propagate from seed and by dividing the plant.

Buphthalmum

Yellow ox-eye

40-60 6-8

Buphthalmum, which literally means cow's eye or ox eye, is derived from the Greek words "bous" (cow) and "opthalmos" (eye). It refers to the shape of the flowers before they have entirely developed.
This profuse, bushy plant from central Europe has erect stems which often branch out. The broad, lanceolote leaves are slightly hairy; the upper leaves are slightly narrower, more delicate and pointed.
B. salicifolium has golden yellow flowers 5-6 cm in diameter on long stems, and willow-like leaves. The plant is suitable for cut flowers.
This is a meadow plant which requires good, lime-rich garden soil. If necessary, support with canes. Regularly removing dead flowers promotes flowering into September. For cut flowers, to prevent wilting, do not cut until the flowers have opened completely. Propagate from seed (spring) or by dividing the plant (autumn).
Attracts bees.

Buphthalmum salicifolium, Yellow ox-eye

Buxus

Box

up to 8 m !

In the past, *Buxus* branches were used on Palm Sunday.
This evergreen, with its small, shiny, leathery leaves, is a very common garden shrub. It is found in all sorts of shapes and is used for hedges. It is easy to prune, and skilful pruning can result in the most diverse shapes, from globes and spirals, to diverse examples of topiary, such as figures of animals.
B. sempervirens from Mediterranean regions, Asia Minor and North America, is extremely suitable for edging, and can also be pruned very easily. The leaves are a narrow or broad oval shape. The foliage is poisonous and has a characteristic sweet smell. Some of the well-known cultivated varieties include: "Aureovariegata" with yellowish-green spotted leaves; "Handsworthensis", a sturdy shrub with dark-green leaves, 4 cm long; "Rotundifolia", with round leaves;

Calamintha

20-80 8-9

Calamintha, an attractive, fragrant plant, derives its name from the Greek "kalos" (beautiful) and "mintha" (mint), and is indigenous from western Europe to central Asia.
The plant has slightly serrated leaves which grow in pairs opposite each other. The clusters of white, pink or lilac, asymmetrical flowers develop in the top leaf axilla.
C. nepata has more or less hairy, round or oval leaves, and ten to twelve white or lilac flowers per cluster. *C. nepata* ssp. *nepeta* has pink flowers. *C. grandiflora* has oval or longer leaves which are less hairy, and slightly larger pink flowers, about five per cluster.
Suitable for rockeries and herb gardens (warm regions), it requires well-drained soil, rich in chalk, heat and sun. Propagate from seed and cuttings.

Buxus box

"Suffruticosa", a dwarf variety with upturned, oval leaves.
Any good, moderately moist garden soil is suitable; protect against drying out; prune in March and again in the summer. Shrubs are available pre-pruned (globe-shaped). For cuttings (in spring), bear in mind the shape that is desired; topping leads to a bushy plant.

Calamintha nepeta ssp. nepeta

Campanula lactiflora "Loddon Anna", Bellflower

Campanula

Bellflower

30-150 6-8

There are many varieties of *Campanula* (which means bell), from low-growing plants which are suitable for rockeries, to tall plants suitable for the backs of borders. It is indigenous in the temperate regions of the northern hemisphere, particularly the Mediterranean region. The five petals of the flowers, which are mainly blue (in every shade) and white, are fused together, often forming a bell, but they are sometimes in the shape of a funnel, tube, dish or star.
C. carpatica flowers from June to September, with sky-blue flowers ("Alba" with white flowers) to a height of 15-30 cm in poor soil. *C. cochlearifolia* has pale-blue/white flowers from June to July, 10-15 cm tall, suitable for rockeries and walls; *C. garganica* has bright blue flowers from May to June, 30 cm tall; *C. lactiflora* has white flowers from June to August, 50-100 cm tall; "Loddon Anna" has pink flowers, 100 cm tall; "Pouffe" has pale blue flowers, 30 cm tall; "Prichard" has amethyst flowers, 60 cm tall; *C. persicifolia* flowers from June to August with very large, broad, bell-shaped pale, bluish-lilac flowers ("Alba", white), 40-100 cm tall; *C. rapunculoides* flowers from May to August with small, pale purple flowers, 30-100 cm tall, suitable for growing wild. In general, the soil should not be too dry (this does not apply for plants that grow in rockeries), well-drained, not too moist in

winter (to prevent rotting). Propagate from seed and cuttings (early summer) and by dividing plants (spring/autumn). Attracts slugs and snails.

Centaurea

Cornflower

30-90 30 7-8

Centaurea is named after the mythological warrior race, the Centaurs (half-man, half-horse). It is indigenous in Mediterranean regions, the Caucasus and Asia Minor, and there are many different shapes and shades as a result of cross-pollination and selection.
C. dealbata grows to a height of 60 cm. It has hairy stems which do not branch

out, and leaves with four parts with straight indentations in the lobes, and smooth edges. It flowers from June to August, with red flowers which are paler or white in the middle, and again in the autumn; "Steenbergi" has purple flowers with a white heart; *C. macrocephala*, 100 cm, flowers from July to August. It has thick stems, with rough, round or long leaves with a serrated edge, and large spherical, thistle-like, golden-yellow flowers, with brown, fringed, involucre leaves. Good for cut flowers; *C. montana*, 50 cm, flowers from May to August, and has silvery-white, hairy, long or oval leaves with smooth edges, and blue flowers with a purple heart. "Alba" has pure white flowers.

Centaurea macrocephala, Cornflower

This plant is easy to grow in any lime-rich, porous soil, not too wet in winter. Propagate from seed (April to May), cuttings or by dividing.

Ceratostigma plumbaginoides

Ceratostigma

20-30 9-10

Ceratostigma is a low-growing shrub from China used for ground cover.
C. plumbaginoides is a bushy plant with slightly woody, reddish stems, reddish-brown leaves in autumn, and gentian blue flowers. The flowers are arranged in compact clusters; the five petals are fused at the bottom to form a narrow tube. The thin stems branch out and are covered with upturned, oval, leathery leaves. The leaves start to turn red before the plant finishes flowering.
C. willmotianum grows to a height of approximately 50 cm and is more sensitive to frost. It is suitable for rockeries and borders. Plant in groups in sandy, lime-rich, nutritious soil which is not too wet.
In severe winters, cover with pine or fir branches. Propagate by dividing plant.

Chelone

Turtle-head

○ ↕ 80-120 ○ ❁ 7-9 ✻ ✂

Chelone means turtle, and this refers to the shape of the upper lip of the flower, which resembles a turtle's shell. This North American plant has sturdy, square stems, and long lanceolate leaves which are fairly deeply indented or serrated. The flowers develop in short, ear-shaped clusters.
The plant can grow to a good size in a few years.
C. obliqua grows to a height of 60 cm, and has fimbriate, crimson flowers suitable for cutting. *C. obliqua* "Alba" has white flowers; *C. lyonii* has pink flowers, and *C. glabra* grows to a height of 1.2 m and has white or pale pink flowers.
Any good garden soil which is not too dry is suitable; manure in spring and autumn. For cut flowers, the bottom flowers in the cluster must be open. Propagate from seed or by dividing the plant. To encourage healthy growth, take up the clumps once every four or five years, dig up the soil, add manure and plant out again.

Chelone obliqua, Turtle-head

Cimicifuga simplex "Braunlaub", Bugbane

Cimicifuga

Bugbane

[○] [↕] 200 [○] [◐] [❁] 8-10 [✻] [!]

The name *Cimicifuga* is derived from the words "cimicis" (bedbug) and "fugare" (drive out); its unpleasant odour repels woodlice and other bugs.
The plant is indigenous in the deciduous woodlands of Europe, North America and central and eastern Asia. It flowers beautifully in autumn and continues to do so until the frost sets in. It is not suitable for cut flowers because of its smell, and also because it is poisonous.
C. acerina (syn. *C. japonica* var. *acerina*) has white flowers which grow in long ears, on thin, erect, leafless stems. The leaves grow in one to three groups of three, and consist of shiny, pointed, deeply indented leaflets with a serrated edge. *C. racemosa* has broad, heart-shaped leaflets and creamy clusters of flowers. *C. simplex* has oval or lanceolate leaflets, and white single clusters of flowers which hang down gracefully.
The plant requires nutritious soil; moist in the shade, or slightly moist in the semi-shade.

Coreopsis grandiflora "Sunray", Tick-seed

Coreopsis

Tick-seed

[○] [↕] 40-100 [○] [❁] 6-9 [✂]

The name *Coreopsis* is derived from the words "koris" (bedbug) and "opsis" (resemble), which refers to the shape of the achene. The genus is indigenous in America and tropical Africa, and comprises annual and perennial plants. The latter are particularly attractive for borders, and are also excellent for cut flowers.
C. grandiflora has erect stems up to 100 cm tall, which usually branch out. The lower leaves are spatulate-shaped with smooth edges; the upper leaves are parted and have narrow leaflets. The beautiful golden-yellow flowers are about 7 cm in diameter and appear from July to August; *C. grandiflora* "Badengold", 100 cm tall, is slightly sturdier; "Sunburst", 100 cm tall, has semi-composite, golden-yellow flowers; "Sunray", 45 cm, has double bright-yellow flowers, *C. lanceolata* has single, lanceolate leaves at the base of the stems, and yellow flowers on its long stems in July and August; "Golden Queen", 60 cm tall, flowers profusely with yellow flowers; "Goldteppich", 25-35 cm tall, has golden-yellow flowers; "Sterntaler", 50 cm tall, golden-yellow with brown spots.
C. verticillata has thin, sturdy stems with no leaves at the base and delicate bipinnate or tripinnate leaves at the top, with narrow leaflets. It grows to a height of 40-60 cm and has small yellow flowers in July to September. Any good, light, porous garden soil which is not too nutritious is suitable.
Propagate from seed and by dividing plants. For compact growth, take up plants every three years, divide and plant out again.

Crambe

Sea kale

75-250 6-7

Crambe is indigenous in Europe, Africa and Asia.
C. cordifolia has greyish, hairy stems and green leaves. The lower leaves are heart-shaped, and the upper leaves have lobes with indented edges. The flower stems are not hairy, and produce large clusters of white flowers in July, protruding above the leaves at a length of 2-2.5 m. *C. maritima* has soft, fleshy, bluish-green stems which branch out and can be eaten as a vegetable when they are blanched. The leaves are large and bluish-green; the lower ones on long stalks are oval with indented edges, the upper ones narrower and smaller.
The whiter clusters of flowers on long stems grow to a height of 75 cm (June/July).
This plant requires sandy, nutritious soil, not too acid, possibly with some lime.
Propagate from seed and cuttings.

Delphinium "New Century Hybrids", Larkspur

Crambe cordifolia, Sea kale

Delphinium

Larkspur

60-180 30-50 6-8

Delphinium is indigenous in temperate and subtropical regions of the northern hemisphere and tropical mountainous regions of Africa.
The asymmetrical flowers have a striking number of stamens in branched or unbranched clusters or ears, and may be in any shade of blue, white, or sometimes pink or yellow. One of the five sepals is elongated to form a long spur.
These elegant plants require a lot of care, but once they flower, it is worth all the trouble.
D. grandiflorum grows to a height of 60-80 cm, and has large, azure, light blue or lilac flowers in July to September. Plant in large groups. *Delphinium* hybrids include Belladonna varieties, Elatum varieties, and the Pacific Giants group. The Belladonna varieties are fairly sturdy and low-growing,

Diascia

• ○ ↕ 10-30 ↔ 10 ○ ✿ 6-9

The name *Diascia* is derived from the Greek "di" (two) and "askos" (bag) because the flowers have two long spurs which contain the nectar. The plant is indigenous in South Africa. It has oval, serrated leaves with rounded ends and forms light clusters of pink flowers on long slender stems. The flowers have a lobed upper lip, and a broad, greatly protruding lower lip with a smooth edge. The two lips are fused to form a deep calyx, which contains four stamens with yellow anthers. The annual, *D. barberae*, grows to a height of 30 cm. Sow at the end of April. *D. cordata* is a perennial dwarf variety, 10-20 cm tall. *D. vigilis* is a perennial bushy plant which is slightly sturdier, flowers profusely, grows to a height of 30 cm and has horizontal and vertical stems. The plant requires well-drained, nutritious soil which retains sufficient moisture. Cover in winter and cut back stems to about 5 cm when the plant has flowered to encourage it to flower again. Propagate from seed. Young plants should be topped when they are 5-6 cm tall, and again when they are 8 cm tall, to encourage flowering. Attracts bees.

up to 100 cm tall, with smaller clusters of flowers which appear in June/July; "Moerheimii" has single white flowers; "Völkerfrieden" has bright gentian flowers. Elatum varieties grow to a height of 125-200 cm and have long clusters of flowers in May/June to July: "Berghimmel" are pale blue with a white centre, "Finsteraarhorn" are a dark gentian blue with a dark centre. The Pacific Giants group, including the "New Century" hybrids, grow to 140 cm and have very large, loose clusters of flowers with large composite flowers; "Black Knight" is a dark violet-blue, "Galahad" is white.
This plant requires some care. It needs fertile, well-drained soil. Manure every year, possibly adding some lime. Plants should be supported with canes to prevent the stems from breaking. Remove dead clusters to encourage flowering. Cut stems when the plants have flowered so that they can flower again - though less profusely - in September. Propagate by dividing plants, from cuttings (spring), and from seed.

Diascia vigilis

Dicentra spectabilis, Bleeding heart

Dicentra

Bleeding heart

○ ↕ 20-80 ◐ ۞ 4-6/5-9 ✳ ✂

This plant is indigenous in North America and eastern Asia. It is also known as Dutchman's Trousers. The name "Bleeding heart" refers to the flowers, particularly of *D. spectabilis*: the two pink outer petals form a sort of heart; the two inner petals are white and resemble a tear.
D. formosa forms low compact clumps of soft, ferny, lightgreen leaves, 20-30 cm tall. It flowers from May to September, with hanging reddish or pale pink clusters, and makes a good border plant. "Alba" has white flowers; "Luxuriant" has purplish-pink flowers. *D. spectabilis*, 60-80 cm, flowers from April to June. It has bluish-green leaves which are grey underneath in double sets of three, and long, elegant hanging flower stems with pink or reddish-pink flowers with a white heart. They are good for cut flowers, flower-beds, in front of shrubs and in window boxes; "Alba" has white flowers. Unfortunately, the plant dies down fairly early on, leaving an empty space.
It requires normal garden soil, rich in humus, and should be protected and transplanted as little as possible. Propagate by dividing plants and from cuttings. Attracts bees.

Digitalis

Foxglove

•• ↕ 50-200 ↔ 20-25 ◐ ۞ 6-8 ✳ ! ✂

The name *Digitalis* is derived from the Latin word, "digitus", which means finger. It refers to the shape of the flower. It is found in Europe, western and central Asia, and is very poisonous; it can even be deadly when eaten. The lower leaves form compact rosettes; the flowers have a tube-shaped, slightly pendant corolla and are arranged in long clusters, usually pointing in the same direction.
D. purpurea has large, long, oval leaves which are hairy on the bottom. The leaves have short stalks or no stalks at all. The numerous flowers are purplish-red, with

Doronicum orientale, Narcissus "Prof. Einstein", Leopard's bane

dark, white edged dots inside. They develop in unbranched clusters up to 70 cm long, which turn to face the sun. There are a large number of cultivated varieties in many colours which are also suitable for cut flowers. "Alba" has white flowers; "Excelsior" has pink flowers pointing in every direction; "Giant Spotted" has white, pale or deep pink flowers; "Sutton's Apricot" has old rose flowers.
This is a woodland plant which grows in any normal garden soil, rich in humus and not too dry. Dead flowers should be removed. For cut flowers, the lowest four or five flowers should be open. Propagate from seed and by dividing plants.

Digitalis purpurea "Giant Spotted", Foxglove

Doronicum

Leopard's bane

○ ↕ 30-80 ◐ ❀ 4-7 ✳ ! ✂

Doronicum is indigenous in Europe, North Africa and Asia. Its beautiful early-flowering yellow flowers are similar to ox-eye daisies. The stems have no or few branches, and the unparted serrated leaves grow at the bottom on long stalks. The leaves are spread out higher up on small stalks and may be more or less hairy; the flowers grow singly or in small groups at the end of long stems.
D. orientale, 30-70 cm, is slightly hairy and has heart-shaped, coarsely serrated leaves and single yellow flowers, approximately 5 cm in diameter. It is good for cut flowers.
D. orientale "Spring Beauty" (syn. "Frühlingspracht"), 50-60 cm, flowers profusely, with composite dark yellow flowers.
This plant grows easily in moist garden soil, rich in humus. Protect against bright sunlight and wind and support if necessary. Remove dead flowers. For cut flowers, the flowers must be half open. Propagate from cuttings after flowering.

Echinacea

Coneflower

75-150 7-9

The name *Echinacea* is derived from the Greek word, "echinos" (sea urchin). The heart of the flower, with its prickly, scale-like bracts, means that these are good for cut flowers, even without ray flowers. This plant is indigenous in North America. It has sturdy, erect stems and spread-out, long, oval, slightly hairy leaves. The single flowers have a brown, yellow or orange heart, and the slightly pendant ray flowers grow on long stems. *E. purpurea* has coarsely serrated leaves which become sparser further up, and purplish-red or white flowers with a dark brown heart, and orangey-yellow styles. For cut flowers the pendant ray flowers are often removed, and only the heart is used. *E. purpurea* "Alba", "White Lustre" and "White Swan" have white ray flowers and a yellowish-brown heart; "Magnus" is whitish-pink.
This plant grows easily in good, normal garden soil. Apply some manure in spring, lift and divide every three years. Remove dead flowers with the stem to encourage growth. Propagate by dividing and from seed.
Attracts butterflies.

Echinacea purpurea, Coneflower

Echinops ritro "Veitch Blue", Globe thistle

Echinops

Globe thistle

80-150 40-60 7-9

The name *Echinops* is derived from the Greek word "echinos" (sea urchin). It has striking, globe-shaped flowers composed of dozens of florets and prickly involucre leaves. This plant is indigenous in eastern and southern Europe, western and central Asia and Africa. The spines can be a nuisance, but nevertheless, the beautiful, long-lasting flowers are excellent for cutting.
E. bannaticus grows to a height of 1 m, and has thick, grey, hairy stems and split pinnate leaves which are greyish-green on

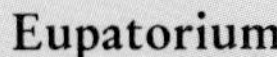

top and a felty grey underneath. The surrounding leaves and petals are bluish-white. "Taplow Blue" flowers profusely with bright blue flowers. *E. ritro*, 50-60 cm, is a bright, steel blue, with split pinnate leaves which are bare on top; "Veitch Blue" is dark blue.
This strong plant likes a fairly dry, light lime-rich soil, not too wet. The distance between plants depends on the variety (height). For cut flowers, the flowers must be two-thirds open; for dried flowers they should not have opened. Propagate by dividing, from seed and from root cuttings. Attracts bees.

Eupatorium

Common Agrimony

150-300 7-9

Not all *Eupatorium* varieties are equally hardy. They are indigenous in Europe, Central and South America, etc. The following varieties are suitable for borders. *E. cannabinum*, 150-200 cm, is hairy with erect, hollow stems and leaves with three to five leaflets in double pairs opposite each other. The flowers grow in umbel-shaped clusters and are a pale pink, red or purple colour. "Album" has white flowers, "Plena" has double, old rose flowers. *E. maculatum*, 150-300 cm, has oval to lanceotale, composite leaves which grow in a ring around the stem; the small purple flowers develop in compact, flat clusters. "Atropurpureum" is a deep purple. *E. purpureum* has pyramid-shaped, purplish-red clusters and makes good cut flowers. *E. rugosum* "Braunlaub", 150 cm, has white flowers which are fairly suitable for cutting.
This plant requires good, fertile soil which is moist and loamy (*E. maculatum*). Support if necessary (against a wall). Propagate by dividing (spring) and by taking cuttings.

Eupatorium rugosum, Common Agrimony

Normal, well-drained garden soil, sufficiently moist. *E. characias* should be protected from the wind. For cut flowers, cut a piece of the stem and stop bleeding by placing the stem in boiling water for a few seconds. Propagate from seed and by dividing plants. Attracts honey-loving insects.

Euphorbia characias ssp. wulfenii, Milkweed

Euphorbia

Milkweed

15-80 5-7

Euphorbia is found all over the world and includes annual as well as perennial plants, succulents, cacti, shrubs and trees, which all contain a toxic, milky sap. The varieties described below are suitable as border plants. The small, unobtrusive flowers are enclosed by brightly coloured leaves which look like petals and determine the plant's decorative value.

E. characias, more than 100 cm tall, has long, oval, greyish-green leaves which grow in a spiral around the thick stems. It has a compact greenish-yellow inflorescence on every stem. *E. griffithii*, 80 cm, has thin, sturdy, slightly bronze-coloured stems with long, narrow, pointed leaves, and a red or yellowish-red inflorescence; "Fire Glow" has bright orange or fiery red flowers suitable for cut flowers, with leaves which turn red and yellow in autumn. *E. polychroma* (syn. *E. epithymoides*), 30-40 cm, has golden-yellow flowers in May-June. It is also suitable for low walls, and cut flowers.

Filipendula

100-200 6-8

Filipendula is found in temperate zones in the northern hemisphere.

This beautiful plant has a wonderful fragrance when it flowers, and finned leaves consisting of two or more serrated, lateral

Filipendula rubra "Venusta"

leaves and a large five or seven-lobed terminal leaf. The flowers grow in profuse, umbellate clusters or plumes and can be pink, purple, white or cream coloured.
F. purpurea, 100 cm, has few lateral leaves and a large, five or seven-lobed serrated, pointed, terminal leaf and pink or crimson spear-shaped clusters of flowers on bare red stems. *F. rubra*, 1-1.5 m, has lateral leaves with lobes, a seven to nine-lobed terminal leaf and small pink plumes; "Venusta", old rose flowers. *F. ulmaria*, 100 cm, has two to five pairs of serrated lateral leaves, a three to five-lobed terminal leaf and a large supporting leaf, and profuse, umbellate, yellowish-white or sometimes pinky-red clusters of flowers. *F. vulgaris*, large elongated leaves with many pairs of deeply indented lateral leaves and large cream or pinky-red flowers.
This plant requires moist soil, *F. vulgaris* slightly drier; manure every spring. If the plant spreads too much, divide into clumps. Propagate from seed and by dividing plant. Attracts bees and beetles.

Fragaria vesca,
Wild strawberry

Fragaria
Wild strawberry

10-20 5-6

Fragaria, derived from the Latin word "fragrum" (fragrant), is a fruiting plant with an attractive scent which is indigenous in Europe, Asia, America and Hawaii. The spherical receptacles are the false fruit - the pips are the true fruit - and have countless stamens and pistils surrounded by five broad, white petals when the plant flowers.
F. vesca has stems with oval, serrated leaves with three lobes, almost all the same length. The stems with white flowers appear above the leaves in May/June, and sometimes flower again in October. The small, round or spherical, bright red fruit has an attractive sweet-sour taste. New plants develop from the long runners which grow above the ground.
Extremely suitable for growing as wild plants and as ground cover. The soil should be rich in humus. The plant propagates itself with runners. They can also be divided. Birds like the receptacles.

moisture-retaining garden soil. Cut back in the autumn, cover with peat; protect in winter. For good, bushy growth, top the plant regularly (until early May) by regularly removing the top pairs of leaves. Water regularly during growth; add manure regularly; remove dead flowers. The plant can be easily propagated by taking (top) cuttings or from seed; in this case, hybrids do not return in a pure form.

Geranium psilostemon

Fuchsia magellanica, Lady's Eardrops

Fuchsia

Lady's Eardrops

100-150 7-10

Fuchsias appear to consist of clusters of bells. They are mainly indigenous in Central and South America and are generally grown in Europe either indoors or in tubs, though there are several hardy varieties which can survive the winter outdoors, and hybrids which also do well in the garden.
The flowers have a long, funnel-shaped calyx-like tube, and four standing or folded back leaflets, and usually four overlapping petals; the stamens (four short, four long), and pistil sometimes protrude from the flower.
F. magellanica, a bushy, tall-growing plant with small, usually serrated leaves in rings; the flowers grow singly or several together in the leaf axilla. They have red sepals and purple petals. There are many cultivated varieties. Hybrids include: "Achievement", with crimson flowers; "Beacon", scarlet and purplish-pink, early flowering; "Chillerton Beauty", pale pink with purple; "Marin Glow", white with purple, flowers profusely; "Royal Purple", deep pink with large, deep purple flowers; "Swingtime", double flowers, scarlet and white; "Ting-a-Ling", entirely white, large, bell-shaped; "Water Nymph", creamy-white with orangey-red. The parts of the plant which are above the ground may die in frost in winter, but soon grow up again in spring. It prefers airy, nutritious, porous,

Geranium

○ ↕ 20-90 ○ ◐ ✿ 5-8 ✳

Following a new classification, the name "geranium" continues to be used for the closely related members of the same family, *Pelargonium*, which can be distinguished by their uneven flowers. The fruit of this plant grows rather like the beak of a bird. *Geranium* is indigenous all over the world, particularly in the cooler regions of the northern hemisphere. It has round flowers with even petals, and there are many varieties, a number of which are suitable for borders, rockeries and small gardens. *G. x cantabrigiense*, 30 cm, flowers from June to July, is aromatic, good for ground cover. It has horizontal stems with light-green, hairless, composite lobed leaves, and five to ten bright lilac-pink flowers on each stem; "Biokovo", 15-20 cm, has pale pink-white or pinkish-red stamens and pistils, in large groups. Take cuttings or divide plants. *G. endressi*, 25-50 cm, flowers in May-July, has horizontal or vertical, slightly hairy stems with hairy, indented, extremely serrated leaves and bright pink, dark-veined upright flowers in double pairs. It flowers again in September. It can spread, or you can propagate it from seed or by dividing the plant. *G. macrorrhizum*, 30-50 cm, flowers in June/July, is aromatic, carpets the ground, and has hairy, erect stems with round, composite, coarsely serrated, prickly leaves and pink, white-veined flowers in double pairs with reddish-brown, swollen calyxes. It prefers a shaded or semi-shaded position and dry soil. Take cuttings, divide or grow from seed. *G. platypetalum*, 40-70 cm, flowers from June to August. It has woolly, hairy, indented, undulating leaves and large attractive bluish flowers in double pairs. The soil should not be too fertile. Propagate from seed or divide the plant. *G. psilostemon*, 40-70 cm, flowers in June and July. It has woolly, hairy, indented, extremely serrated leaves and large, attractive bright purplish-red flowers with black veins and a black heart. Support plant in well-drained soil. Divide and sow. *G. sanguineum*, 15-25 cm, flowers in June and July. It is sturdy and has hairy, branching stems with shiny, dark-green parted leaves. It flowers profusely with large, blood-red flowers. It can tolerate dry conditions. Divide plants or sow seeds. In general, nutritious soil, slight shade, support taller varieties.

Geranium macrorrhizum

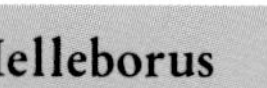

Helleborus orientalis, Stinking hellebore

Helleborus

Stinking hellebore

30-80 40-70 12-4 !

Helleborus is poisonous and is indigenous in Europe and Asia Minor. It flowers in winter and early spring. The parted leathery leaves develop from the root, or grow singly on the stems. The large flowers have white, red or green sepals and many small honeycomb-shaped petals. *H. argutifolius*, 80 cm, November-March/April, has thick, branching stems with many bluish-green, three-lobed, prickly serrated leaves and a large number of pale greenish-yellow clusters of flowers hanging forwards. *H. foetidus*, Stinking hellebore, 80 cm, March-April, has smaller, narrow, bright green serrated leaflets; the top leaf on the stem is unparted. It has pendent, bell-shaped flowers which are light green with a reddish-brown edge, and exudes a smell if damaged. *H. niger*, the Christmas Rose, 30 cm, December-April, has parted root leaves, is unbranched, has virtually no leaves on the stems, and has white - and later, pink - dish-shaped flowers.

H. orientalis, 50 cm, January-April, has fan-shaped root leaves with soft hair on the bottom, numerous hanging stems with three or more dish-shaped white, pink or red flowers.

This is a solitary plant which likes lime-rich soil, rich in humus. It should be protected and left alone as far as possible. Do not remove leaves which have been shed. Propagate by dividing and from seed. Attracts bees.

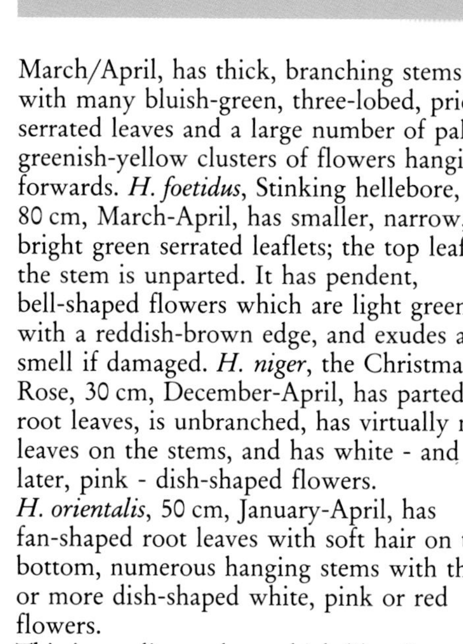

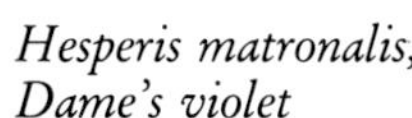

Hesperis matronalis, Dame's violet

Hemerocallis

Day lily

60-100 40-60 6-8

The name *Hemerocallis* is derived from the Greek words, "hemera" (day) and "kallos" (beautiful). The attractive flowers blossom briefly, but there are so many on a stem in various stages of development that the plant flowers for a long time. It is indigenous in the temperate zones of Asia and Europe, and cross-pollination has resulted in many beautiful flowering hybrids which thrive even in less favourable spots.

The grass-like leaves form attractive, sturdy clumps; the sturdy round stems usually protrude above these. The original star-shaped flowers vary greatly in shape and colour as a result of selection.

H. citrina, 70-100 cm, has lemon-yellow fragrant flowers. *H. middendorfii*, 30-60 cm, May-June, has fragrant buttercup yellow to orangey-yellow flowers. Hybrids include "Beppie" and "Bonanza", 70 cm, bright yellow and brown; "Corky", 80 cm, reddish-brown buds and lemon-yellow flowers; "Icecap", 80 cm, pale yellow; "Pink Damast", 80 cm, pink with a white stripe; "Sammy Russell", 70 cm, deep brownish-red with a whitish-yellow stripe. Any nutritious moist soil is suitable. Add well-rotted manure if necessary. When the plants decline, lift, divide and plant out again. Propagate by dividing in spring.

Hesperis

Dame's Violet

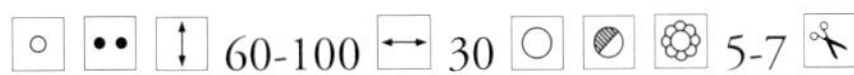

60-100 30 5-7

The name *Hesperis* comes from the Greek word "hespera" (of the evening). The flowers are beautifully scented in the evening and attract countless moths; "Sweet Rocket" is another appropriate name. The plant originates from Mediterranean regions and northern and western Asia. It is usually treated as a biennial because the flowering declines significantly after a few years.
The broadly serrated, long, lanceolate leaves taper to a point, and are spread over the stems; the light purple or white flowers have four sepals and four petals and grow in clusters. *H. matronalis*, 80-100 cm, has long pinkish-violet clusters of flowers. "Alba" has white flowers. *H. steviana*, 40-70 cm, is more compact, with hairy, greyish-green leaves and light pinkish-violet flowers.
The plant is suitable for growing wild in normal fertile garden soil, not too acid. Remove dead flowers to encourage new buds to develop (into the autumn). For cut flowers, a few of the flowers in the cluster must be open. Propagate from seed.

Hemerocallis "Beppie", Day lily

Heuchera

Palace Purple

30-60 6-8

The luxuriant light inflorescences of *Heuchera*, which is indigenous in North America, come into their own when they are planted in large groups together.
The leaves of this plant are arranged on stalks in a rosette and remain green for a long time. The small, bell-shaped, red, pink or white flowers develop on elegant stems from these rosettes.
H. micrantha has fairly large, broad, irregular lobed leaves with a wavy edge and pink flowers: "Purple Palace", 50 cm, has large leaves, purplish-brown on the upper side and dark red on the underside, and cream-coloured inflorescences. *H. sanguinea* has dark green heart-shaped or round lobed leaves with an undulating edge and long stems with blood-red flowers; "Splendens", 60 cm, May-July, is pinkish-red. Hybrids include "Pluie de Feu", 50 cm, which flowers profusely with deep red flowers; "Schneewittchen", 40 cm, white.
This plant requires porous garden soil, rich in humus and not too heavy. Keep moist and add some compost. Cover when there is severe frost, and when the plant declines, lift it, divide and plant out again. For cut flowers, half of the flowers must be open. Propagate by dividing the plant.

Heuchera micrantha "Palace Purple"

Hosta sieboldiana "Elegans"

Hosta

○ ↕ 30-60 ◐ ● ❀ 7-8

Hosta grows wild in Japan, but there are many cultivated varieties resulting from a process of selection. Both the leaves and flowers are attractive. Rosettes of broad, unparted, green or variegated veined leaves develop from the large rootstock and the stems with pendent funnel-shaped clusters of flowers grow from these.
H. x fortunei , 60 cm, has green, lanceolate leaves and pale purple flowers; "Albopicta" (syn. "Aureomaculata") has yellowish or yellowish-white young leaves with dark green edges which later turn an even darker green. *H. lancifolia*, 30-75 cm, has lanceolate, pointed green leaves and stems with about twenty violet, bell-shaped, slightly pendent flowers placed at regular intervals. *H. plantaginea*, 75 cm, has heart-shaped, shiny, greenish-yellow, beautifully veined leaves and compact clusters of large white, lily-like, fragrant flowers. *H. sieboldiana*, 75 cm, has oval or heart-shaped, bluish-green attractively veined leaves, and white clusters of flowers; "Elegans" has undulating greyish-blue leaves. This is an easy plant to grow as ground cover in moist, nutritious soil with some leaf mould or peat. The variegated varieties should be planted in semi-shade, and lifted every four or five years. The young plants should be planted out again in soil which has been dug over and manured. Propagate

by dividing (spring/autumn) and from seed (spring).
Attracts slugs; the holes made by slugs grow with the leaves, so that they become less attractive.

Iberis

↕ 20-30 ○ ❀ 5-6 ✳

It comes as no surprise to learn that *Iberis* originates from the Iberian peninsula, but it is indigenous in North Africa and western Asia, as well as Spain and Portugal, and comprises both annual and perennial plants.

I. sempervirens is an evergreen, compact shrub, hardy in winter, with elongated, lanceolate or spatulate flat leaves with smooth edges and umbels of white flowers. These umbels grow longer as the plant flowers. "Findel", 20 cm, has large white flowers; "Snowflake" flowers profusely with white flowers. There are also pink and purple varieties.
This plant requires moist lime-rich soil, not too wet and a sheltered position. To protect against frost, cover with pine branches or straw. Prune the shrubs as soon as they have flowered to encourage compact growth and prevent then from becoming bare.
Propagate from cuttings in summer, by dividing, and from seed.

Incarvillea delavayi

Incarvillea

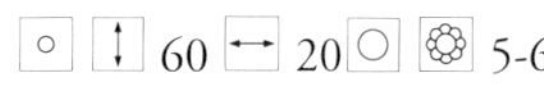
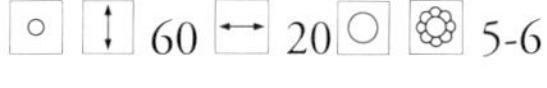

60 20 5-6

Incarvillea is named after the Jesuit, d'Incarville, who sent seeds from China to Europe. It is indigenous in central Asia and the Himalayas. The leaves of this plant are unparted or have four lobes and a serrated edge. The bell-shaped flowers are grown singly or in clusters.
I. delavayi (after Father Delavay, a member of D'Incarville's order) has single, pinnate, serrated leaves, 30-50 cm long, which grow in a rosette. The purplish-pink flowers growing in clusters of three or more together have a yellow tube-shaped corolla and two upper petals smaller than the rest. The plant requires lime-rich, sandy, nutritious, porous soil. It is susceptible to standing water (root rot). Protect by covering well in winter. Propagate from seed (April-May for flowers in the following year).

Iberis sempervirens

Iris

Iris

60-125 8-10 5-7

In Greek mythology, Iris (Rainbow) was the beautiful, fleet-footed messenger between the gods and man. There are hundreds of varieties of these bulbs in all sorts of colours. They are perennials and marsh plants, and are indigenous in the northern hemisphere. The stems are erect and sometimes branch out with narrow, long or sword-shaped, overlapping leaves with clear veins running the length of the leaves. One flower or small groups of flowers with three standing and three pendent, hairless or hairy petals (bearded iris) develop at the end of the stems. Perennial irises form rootstocks. *I. germanica*, 60-100 cm, is a bearded iris which flowers in May. It has bluish-green leaves, light and dark purplish-blue petals with a white beard. There are many excellent hybrids, including "Ambassadeur", which is bronze-violet with purple; "Blue Rhythm" is pure blue; "Dancer's Veil" is white with a purple edge; "Die Braut" is low-growing with white flowers; "Earl of Essex" is purplish-blue and white; "Granada Gold" is yellow; "Imperator" is a reddish-violet; "Ola Kala" is dark yellow; "Susan Bliss" is pink; "White Knight" is white. *I. pumila*, 10-15 cm, a dwarf iris, flowers in April-May, with yellow, violet or dark blue flowers; "Meadow Court" is a bronze colour with yellow. *I. sibirica* and hybrids, 70-100 cm, are beardless irises which flower in June with large clumps of grass-like bluish leaves with a wine-red base and flowers ranging from purplish-blue to white. Irises require dry, lime-rich, well-drained soil; *I. germanica* and *I. pumila*, not too moist. *I. sibirica* also thrives by ponds. Propagate by dividing rootstock and sow.

Kirengeshoma palmata,
Japanese wax flower

Kirengeshoma

Japanese wax flower

75-90 50 8-9

Kirengeshoma is indigenous in Japan and Korea. The name is a Japanese reference to the similar genus, *Anemonopsis*. The beautiful flowers have a waxy structure, and the attractive leaves remain on the plant for a long time after it has finished flowering. *K. palmata* is a sturdy, leafy plant with

Left:
Iris germanica
"Earl of Essex"

purplish stems and large, slightly hairy leaves opposite each other, with deeply indented, lobed leaf edges. The leaf stalks become shorter further up the plant. The pale yellow nodding flowers are bell-shaped and are arranged in loosely composed clusters. *K. koreana* (syn. *K. palmata* var. *koreana*) is almost identical. It grows slightly larger and flowers earlier.
This plant requires moist, nutritious soil, rich in humus, not too heavy. Add some compost. Propagate by dividing and from cuttings (spring).

Knautia

Scabious

○ ↕ 50-100 ○ ❁ 5-9 ✳

Knautia is indigenous in Europe. It is recommended as a remedy against scurvy, and used to be classified under the closely related genus, *Scabiosa.* It comprises annual and perennial plants.
The plant has broad, deeply indented, hairy leaves growing opposite each other, and spherical flowers on stems which branch out.
K. arvensis is an extremely diverse variety and is found growing wild on roadside verges and railway cuttings. It has lanceolate leaves growing smaller further up, and lilac or bright blue, slightly scented flowers.
K. macedonia has striking, large, purplish-violet flowers.
This is an easy plant to grow in normal, well-drained garden soil, and is also suitable for growing wild. Propagate from seed.

Knautia macedonia

Lavandula angustifolia,
Lavender,
and Stachys byzantina

Lavatera olbia "Rosea"

Lavandula

Lavender

30-60 7-8

The name *Lavandula* comes from the Latin word "lavare", to wash, clean. It used to be added to bath water and is still used in toiletries, soap, perfume, and dried in the linen cupboard.
This fragrant plant is indigenous in Mediterranean regions, Portugal, the Canary Islands and Madeira.
L. angustifolia, 60 cm, has stiff, thin, erect stems with greyish-green, spatulate or elongated leaves which grow opposite each other, and blue flowers in long ears. "Alba", 50 cm, has greyish-white flowers; "Dwarf Blue", 25-40 cm, is lilac; "Hidcote", 30-40 cm, is a deep violet-blue; "Munstead", 30 cm, is lilac; "Rosea", 40 cm, is pinky-lilac.
This plant thrives in poor, fairly dry, lime-rich, porous soil. It should be sheltered and not too wet in winter. Cut back as soon as it has finished flowering to prevent the plant looking bare and to encourage bushy growth. Propagate from cuttings in summer (not from woody twigs).
Attracts insects, special bees and butterflies.

Lavatera

Tree mallow

80-200 7-10

Lavatera is indigenous mainly in Mediterranean regions. It comprises annual and biennial plants as well as perennial (semi-) shrubs.
The plant often has hairy, lobed or angular leaves, and clusters of large, hibiscus-like flowers with five, wide-open petals.
L. olbia is an evergreen shrub which branches out dramatically and has pink flowers; "Rosea", 150-200 cm, has hairy, three to five-lobed leaves, and large pink flowers on short stems. *L. thuringiaca* has oval or lanceolate, three-lobed serrated leaves, and pale, pinkish-red flowers: "Barnsley" has strikingly large, pinkish-red flowers.
This plant thrives in any good, porous, not too fertile or moist soil in a sheltered position. Protect in winter by covering with straw. Propagate from cuttings in August/September. Winter in a light, cool place. Plant out in March.

Leucanthemum x superbum "Noordlicht", Ox-eye daisy

Leucanthemum

Ox-eye daisy

50-100 5-8

The name *Leucanthemum* is derived from the Greek words "leukos" (white) and "anthemon" (flower), which refer to the radiant white petals. Until recently it was classified under *Chrysanthemum*, though this now includes only annual plants.
L. x superbum (syn. *L. maximum*, *Chrysanthemum maximum*) is indigenous in the Pyrenees. It grows to a height of 60 cm, has hairless, unbranched stems, serrated, indented leaves, which have stalks and are a spatulate shape at the bottom, while at the top they become smaller and lanceolate or elongated. The single flowerheads are 7-8 cm in diameter with white outer petals and a yellow heart. There are beautiful white and composite varieties, such as "Alaska", "Giant", "Noordlicht" ("Polaris"), "Wirral Supreme", "Zilverprinses".
L. vulgare is indigenous in Europe. It has hairless, erect stems. The lower leaves have long stalks and are an oval shape, becoming longer towards the top. The leaves are serrated or lobed, and the top leaf has a smooth edge with a long stalk. The plant has single white flowers with a yellow heart.
The plant thrives in any good, fertile, moist soil suitable for meadow flowers. Propagate from seed, or cultivated varieties by dividing the plant. Lift clumps every three years. Divide and plant out the new sections.

Liatris

○ ↕ 50-150 ○ ❁ 7-9 ✂

The flowering ears of *Liatris*, which originates from North America, flower from top to bottom, in contrast with most plants. It has erect stems which hardly branch out, and narrow, unparted leaves which are close together. The long, compact, flowering ears are composed of single, tube-shaped, pinkish-red, pinkish-violet or white flowers.
L. pycnostachya, 90-150 cm, has long, narrow leaves which become shorter further up, and compact, purple flowering ears on hairy stems. *L. spicata*, 50-100 cm, has narrow, lanceolate leaves and huge purple flowering ears on hairless stems: "Alba" has white flowers; "Kobold", 50-60 cm, has compact, bluish-mauve flowering ears. This plant should be planted in groups in well-drained, not too wet soil in a sheltered position; *L. pycnostachya* also thrives in very dry soil; *L. spicata* is more resistant to moisture. For cut flowers, the top flowers in the ear must be open. Propagate by dividing or from seed.

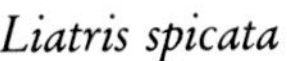
Liatris spicata

Ligularia

○ ↕ 80-150 ◐ ❁ 6-9 ❄ ✂

The name *Ligularia* comes from the Latin word "ligula" (tape), which refers to the long, outer petals of the flowerhead. It is sometimes mistaken for *Senecio*. It is indigenous in the temperate regions of Asia, and definitely requires moist soil.
This plant has large decorative rosettes of leaves, consisting of big, heart-shaped coarsely serrated or indented leaves with long stalks. The long, sturdy stems, with yellow or orange clusters of flowers, ears or umbels develop from these rosettes.
L. dentata, 100-150 cm, has large, bright green serrated leaves, thick stems which branch out at the top and have dark, orangey-yellow flowers in broad, loose

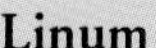

umbels: "Othello" has dark-green leaves, dark red at the bottom, and orangey-red umbels of flowers. *L. przewalskii*, 150 cm, has deeply indented, parted leaves, and long, narrow, ear-shaped yellow clusters of flowers on slender stems. It is suitable for growing wild. *L. veitchiana*, 150-200 cm, has extremely large, heart-shaped leaves and long, slender, bright yellow ears of flowers. These plants grow in groups or singly in moist nutritious soil, rich in humus, and require a great deal of room. Propagate from seed and by dividing (spring). Attracts bees, butterflies and insects.

Linum

Flax

20-100 6-8

Linum is indigenous in temperate regions all over the world. It has been cultivated as flax since time immemorial, and comprises annual, biennial and perennial plants. It flowers profusely and has thin stems, long, narrow leaves, and bright blue, red, yellow or white loose clusters of flowers.

L. flavum, 50 cm, has spatulate or lanceolate bluish-green leaves and branching plumes of flowers with dish-shaped bright yellow flowers: "Compactum", 30 cm, flowers profusely with yellow flowers. *L. narbonense*, 30-50 cm, has slender stems, bright green, narrow lanceolate leaves, and numerous violet blue flowers. *L. perenne*, 50-70 cm, has very slender stems, long or lanceolate, narrow bluish-green leaves and masses of sky blue, wide-open flowers with a yellow heart: "Diamond" has white flowers; "Saphir" is bright blue.
This plant thrives in any well-drained, moist garden soil in a warm, sunny position. Support with canes or neighbouring plants. It is not suitable for cut flowers. Propagate from seed and cuttings.
Attracts bees.

Left:
Linum perenne, Flax

Ligularia dentata
"Othello"

Lobelia

○ ↕ 50-100 ◉ ✿ 7-8

Lobelia originates mainly from tropical and subtropical regions. There is an enormous diversity of varieties, including annual and perennial plants which all like wet conditions. The leaves of the plant are spread out, and it has red, blue, yellow or white flowers which grow singly or in plumes, with uneven lobed petals. *L. fulgens* has thin leafy stems, small, long, lanceolate leaves and bright red plumes of flowers. It is not entirely winter-hardy: "Queen Victoria", 80-100 cm, has brownish-red leaves and blood-red plumes. *L. x gerardii*, 80 cm, has purple flowers. *L. siphilitica* has sturdy, erect stems, long, lanceolate, serrated leaves and slender, deep blue or purple plumes of flowers. It is hardy in winter; "Alba" has white plumes of flowers.

The plant requires moist, nutritious soil, organic manure. it is also very suitable by ponds and streams; *L. fulgens* may be dug up to spend the winter in a frost-free place. Propagate from seed and by dividing plants (in spring).

Lobelia siphilitica and L.s. "Alba", Lobelia

Lunaria annua, Honesty

Lunaria

Honesty

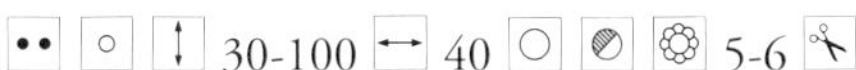

The name *Lunaria* comes from the Latin word "luna" (moon), which refers to the translucent, silvery, round seed partitions. It is indigenous in central and southeast Europe. *L. annua* grows wild in western Europe and is usually cultivated as a biennial plant. It has thin, branching stems, heart-shaped serrated leaves; the lower leaves have long stalks, the upper leaves grow directly from the stem. It has lilac, purple or white flowers; "Alba" has white flowers; "Purpurea" has dark pink flowers; "Variegata" has variegated leaves with white edges and white flowers. After flowering in May-June, the fruit or discs remain on the plant until winter.
The plant requires moist soil, not too poor. Tie up when it is flowering. To dry the honesty, at the end of the summer cut the stems just above the ground and hang upside down, out of the sun. When they have been dried, any brown covers can be carefully removed. Propagate from seed (April/May) and by dividing the plant. Attracts bees.

Lychnis

Maltese Cross

30-100 15-25 6-8

The name *Lychnis* is derived from the Greek word "lychnos" (lamp), which refers to the bright colour of the flower. It is indigenous in the temperate zones of Europe and America and in the polar region.
L. chalcedonica, 60-100 cm, has erect, hairy stems, light green, coarse-haired, long, oval leaves with a heart-shaped base, small bright red flowers in compact umbels; "Alba" has white flowers; "Carnea" has pale pink flowers; "Rosea" has pinky-red flowers.
L. viscaria, 30-60 cm, has reddish, virtually unbranched, sticky stems, spatulate, pointed, hairless leaves, and short-stemmed crimson flowers in narrow, airy plumes; "Alba", 50 cm tall, flowers profusely with white flowers and has pale green leaves; "Plena", 40 cm, has composite, pinkish-red flowers; "Splendens", 50 cm, has large red flowers.
This is an easy plant to grow in any type of soil. It makes good cut flowers. Propagate from seed (July-August) and by dividing plants (August-September). Lift plants every three to four years after they have flowered. Divide and plant out new sections in well-dug, airy soil, after adding some compost.

Lychnis chalcedonica, Maltese Cross

Malva moschata "Alba", Mallow

Lysimachia

Loosestrife

5-90 6-9

Lysimachia is indigenous in Europe, North America and eastern Asia. It comprises many totally different varieties, and if you are not careful, the creeping rootstock can take up a lot of room.
L. clethroides, 60-90 cm, June to August, has bluish-green, slightly hairy, long, oval leaves with short stalks and compact white flowers in long, elegantly curved, hanging ears. It is good for cut flowers. *L. nummularia*, 5 cm, June-July, grows rapidly and makes good ground cover in moist spots. It has bright green, almost round leaves with smooth edges and short stalks, and single, golden-yellow flowers in the leaf axilla.
L. punctata, 30-60 cm, flowers in June to August, and has dense foliage and slightly hairy, erect stems and oval or lanceolate leaves in rings with virtually no stalks. It has clusters of golden-yellow, star-shaped flowers which grow erect in the leaf axilla, making good cut flowers.
This plant spreads rapidly in moist soil, rich in humus. Remove young shoots and parts of the rootstock to inhibit growth. For cut flowers, the first flowers should be open. Propagate from seed and cuttings and by dividing the plant. Attracts bees.

Lysimachia punctata, Loosestrife

Malva

Mallow

30-120 6-9

Malva is indigenous in Europe, Asia and Africa. It has been used for centuries as a medicinal herb and as a vegetable, eaten cooked or raw. It comprises annual and perennial varieties.

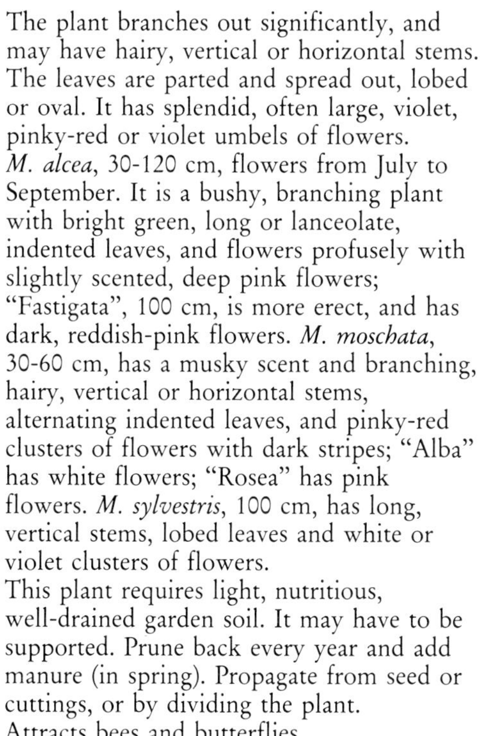

The plant branches out significantly, and may have hairy, vertical or horizontal stems. The leaves are parted and spread out, lobed or oval. It has splendid, often large, violet, pinky-red or violet umbels of flowers.
M. alcea, 30-120 cm, flowers from July to September. It is a bushy, branching plant with bright green, long or lanceolate, indented leaves, and flowers profusely with slightly scented, deep pink flowers; "Fastigata", 100 cm, is more erect, and has dark, reddish-pink flowers. *M. moschata*, 30-60 cm, has a musky scent and branching, hairy, vertical or horizontal stems, alternating indented leaves, and pinky-red clusters of flowers with dark stripes; "Alba" has white flowers; "Rosea" has pink flowers. *M. sylvestris*, 100 cm, has long, vertical stems, lobed leaves and white or violet clusters of flowers.
This plant requires light, nutritious, well-drained garden soil. It may have to be supported. Prune back every year and add manure (in spring). Propagate from seed or cuttings, or by dividing the plant.
Attracts bees and butterflies.

Meconopsis

Blue poppy

30-120 5-10 !

The name *Meconopsis* is derived from the Greek words "mekon" (poppy) and "opsis" (resemble), because it resembles a poppy. It is mainly indigenous in Asia.
This plant has beautiful rosettes of leaves and striking, bright colours.
M. betonicifolia, 100 cm, flowers from June to August. It has greyish-green compact rosettes of long, oval, fimbriate leaves and sturdy stems with several sky-blue, slightly pendent flowers. *M. cambrica*, 20-30 cm, flowers from May to August. It has composite, bushy, fresh green leaves which are bluish-green underneath. There are many stems, each with single, yellow, poppy-like flowers.
This is rather a difficult plant which requires slightly acid, moist, well-drained soil, rich in humus. Add organic manure and do not allow to dry out in summer. Cover lightly in winter as the plant may rot if it is too wet. *M. cambrica* is easier and not so demanding. Propagate from seed or by dividing plants.

Meconopsis betonicifolia,
Blue poppy

Mimulus "Queen's Price", Monkey Musk

Monarda

Bergamot

80-120 7-9

Monarda comes from North America. It has beautifully fragrant flowers which grow in a curious way: a new bud can develop in the middle of the flowering head and the flowers grow one on top of the other.
The plant has erect, square stems, round, long or oval serrated leaves opposite each other, and spherical clusters of large pink, bright-red or white flowers.
M. didyma, 60-100 cm, has numerous vertical stems which may be hairy and branch out, oval, pointed serrated leaves, red flowerheads with a collar of reddish bracts. *M. fistulosa* has smaller leaves, and violet or lilac-pink flowers with purple bracts. *Monarda* "Adam" has cherry-red flowers; "Blaustrumpf" has bluish-purple stems and dark lilac flowers; "Cambridge Scarlet" has deep scarlet flowers; "Croftway Pink" flowers profusely with pale pink flowers; "Fishes" has large, white-pink flowers with

Mimulus

Monkey Musk

20-30 6-9

Mimulus is indigenous in North America. In the past, it deserved its name, but unfortunately it has lost its fragrance in the course of time. This is a vertical-growing or spreading plant, which may be hairy or hairless, with leaves which may or may not be serrated or lobed, and with beautiful, trumpet-shaped flowers.
M. guttatus has hairy, unbranched stems, long, oval serrated leaves with or without stalks, and yellow clusters of flowers with brown or purplish-red spots. *M. luteus* has creeping, hairless stems, broad, oval, serrated leaves, and yellow, red, or purple spotted flowers which are wide open in loose clusters. *M. moschatus* lies partly on the ground, and has soft, hairy stems, long, oval leaves with short stalks, sometimes serrated, and pale yellow flowers, spotted with light brown. Hybrids are often cultivated as annuals. "Major Bees" has large yellow flowers spotted with red; "Orange Glow" is orangey-red; "Queen's Price" is white and yellow with red spots. This plant requires moist, nutritious soil. Cover with pine branches in winter. Propagate from seed, cuttings or by dividing (in October).

a green heart; "Prärienacht" has lilac-purple flowers; "Schneewittchen" has white flowers. Plant in large groups in strong, moist garden soil. It is sensitive to dry conditions, but must not be too wet in winter (root rot). It is susceptible to mildew. Remove dead flowers. Divide plant every two or three years. For cut flowers, the flowers must be half open. Propagate by dividing plants and from seed. It attracts butterflies, flies and bees.

Nepeta x faassenii "Little Tich", Catmint

Monarda didyma "Cambridge Scarlet", Bergamot

Nepeta

Catmint

○ ↕ 30-100 ○ ✿ 6-8

The fragrant plant, *Nepeta*, is indigenous in the temperate and subtropical regions of Europe, Asia and North Africa. It does not attract only insects, but as its name suggests, cats also make use of this plant. It has greyish, hairy stems, serrated or indented leaves, opposite each other, and an ear-shaped inflorescence of pale pink, lilac or dark-blue flowers, growing one above the other in rings.

N. x faassenii, 30-50 cm, has hairy, branching stems, small, greyish-green serrated leaves and beautiful lilac clusters of flowers; "Blauknirps" has bluish-purple flowers; "Six Hills Giant", 40-60 cm, is a deeper purplish-blue; "Snowflake" is white-blue; "Little Tich" is pink or lilac-blue. *N. govaniana*, 60-80 cm, has thin, branching stems, pale green lemon-scented leaves and yellowish-white flowers.

N. sibirica, 100 cm, is a spreading plant with lanceolate leaves and lavender flowers. The plant requires good, porous, normal, rather dry garden soil. Cover lightly in winter and support with neighbouring plants if necessary. *N. govaniana* tolerates more moisture. *N. sibirica* should be regularly cut back to stop it spreading. Cut the stems when the plant has flowered to encourage a second flowering. Propagate from seed and by dividing the plant.

Attracts bees and butterflies.

Nicotiana sylvestris, Flowering Tobacco

Omphalodes

American forget-me-not

15-20 4-5

Omphalodes is indigenous in Mediterranean regions, Asia and Mexico. It looks rather like the forget-me-not, though it is not clear why it should be known as the "American" forget-me-not.

The plant forms clumps and has broad, oval, long, pointed leaves, erect or horizontal stems, and sky-blue or white flowers in loose clusters.

O. cappadocica has fresh green clumps of tightly-packed leaves with coarse hair and long stalks, and small, bluish-violet flowers. *O. verna* has more delicate hairy leaves, larger blue flowers with a white heart, and is used for ground cover; "Alba" has white flowers.

This plant is easy to grow and tends to spread (*O. verna*). It thrives in any moist soil, rich in humus. New shoots can be removed. Propagate from seed and by dividing plants.

Omphalodes cappadocica, American forget-me-not

Nicotiana

Flowering Tobacco

40-100 25-30 6-9 !

Nicotiana, which is indigenous in North and South America, is usually cultivated as an annual for decorative purposes.

This is a sticky, hairy plant with undulating leaves and funnel-shaped or trumpet-shaped white, red, green or yellow flowers which are beautifully scented in the evening, but hang down limply in the sun during the day. *N. alata* "Grandiflora" (syn. *N. affinis*) has erect stems, oval or long, lanceolate leaves, yellowish-white flowers with long, tubular petals which are closed during the daytime but open in the evening and have a beautiful scent; "Lime Green" has greenish-yellow flowers; "Sensation" has mixed colours and is open in the daytime. *N. silvestris*, 150 cm, has violin-shaped leaves and nodding, white, beautifully scented flowers with long, white tubular petals in plumes, which remain open in cloudy weather.

This plant requires fertile, moist soil, not too wet. Propagate from seed (sow indoors in March-April, plant out at the end of May) and from cuttings.

Attracts butterflies and moths.

Origanum vulgare "Compactum", Marjoram

Origanum

Marjoram

○ ↕ 40-60 ↔ 15-20 ○ ❁ 6-9 ✻

The name *Origanum* is derived from the Greek words "oros" (mountain) and "ganos" (joy). It is indigenous in particular in Mediterranean regions where it is found on hills and mountain slopes. It has many culinary and medicinal uses. This plant has bushy, branching stems, leaves opposite each other, and many small, white, pink and lilac flowers. *O. laevigatum*, 40 cm, July to October, has thin branching stems and slender lilac-purple plumes of flowers; "Album" has white flowers; "Herrenhausen" is a stiffer plant with sturdy stems, dark-green leaves and compact lilac plumes of flowers. *O. vulgare*, 30-60 cm, has bushy, branching stems and flowers from July to September. It has hairy, green, slightly serrated leaves, and thick plumes of small pink or white flowers; "Aureum", 25 cm, has golden-yellow leaves and pale pink flowers; "Compactum", 15 cm, is used for ground cover, and has small, dark-green leaves and lilac-pink flowers; "Thumble's Variety", 30 cm, flowers from July to August. It has golden-yellow or yellowish-green leaves far into the autumn, and pale pink flowers. Hybrids include "Erntedank", 50 cm, which is less compact and has loose, dark lilac-purple plumes of flowers; "Nymphemburg", 50 cm, is bushier with dark-green leaves and many pale, lilac-pink flowers.

This plant requires good, well-drained, lime-rich, rather dry garden soil. Cover lightly in winter. Propagate by dividing plants. It attracts bees and butterflies.

Perovskia

100-150 8-9

Perovskia, is indigenous in Asia, and one of the few shrubs which flowers in autumn. It is a fragrant semi-shrub with delicate square stems, small leaves which grow in pairs and slender plumes of narrow, purplish-blue flowers.
P. atriplicifolia has greyish-white, felted, hairy stems, greyish-green lanceolate leaves with short stalks, and coarsely serrated edges, and lilac-blue, ear-shaped plumes of flowers which stand up straight at first, but gradually droop; "Blue Spire" and "Blue Haze" have beautiful, purplish-blue plumes of flowers.
This is an attractive shrub to use in the border between low-growing plants and ground cover. It is treated as a perennial. The shoots, which die off in winter, run out in spring. It requires lime-rich, well-drained soil and a slightly sheltered position.
Cut back in spring to just above the ground for better flowers. Protect slightly against frost. Propagate by dividing plant, from seed or cuttings.

Perovskia atriplicifolia "Blue Spire"

Phlox

Phlox

30-120 5-9

The name *Phlox* comes from the Greek word "phlox" (flame). With its fragrant, brightly coloured flowers, it can be used to fill an entire border. The genus is mainly indigenous in North America.
The plant has creeping or vertical stems, with irregularly placed leaves with short stalks or no stalks, and beautifully coloured plumes or umbels of flowers.
P. x arendsii, "Anja", 40-60 cm, flowers from May to August. It has vertical branching stems with purplish-red flowers; "Hilda" has white and pale lilac flowers with a pink heart; "Suzanne" has white flowers with a red heart. *P. divaricata*, 30-40 cm, flowers from May to June. It is a creeping plant with oval leaves and lilac or lavender-blue clusters of flowers; "Blue Dreams" has blue flowers; "Dirigo Ice" has white flowers. *P. paniculata*, 90-180 cm,

Phlox paniculata "Bright Eyes", Phlox

flowers from July to September. It has long, oval leaves with virtually no stalks, and white or pink plumes of flowers. There are many hybrids varying in height, colour and time of flowering. *P. stolofinera*, 20-30 cm, flowers from April to May. It is a creeping plant which carpets the ground with rosettes of oval or spatulate leaves with stalks, vertical stems and red or purplish-red flowers: "Blue Ridge" has purplish-blue flowers; "Irridescens" has lavender-blue flowers.
This plant requires good, well-dug, fertile garden soil which retains moisture, but is not too wet. Add manure in spring. It is susceptible to fungus on the leaves.
For cut flowers, a few flowers should be open. Propagate from seed or cuttings, or divide plants.

Physostegia

60-120 7-9

Phystostegia is indigenous in North America. It has pyramid-shaped inflorescences like ears; the flowers can be turned individually (not too far) and left in that position.
This plant forms clumps with thin vertical stems, pairs of lanceolate leaves, and stiff, pyramid-shaped inflorescences like ears of white or purplish-red flowers.
P. virginiana has vertical, square stems, lanceolate, strongly serrated leaves with or without stalks, and pink flowers; "Alba", "Summer Snow" and "Snow Spire" have white flowers; "Bouquet Rose" is a beautiful pink; "Red Beauty" is red; "Vivid" is pinkish red.
This is an easy plant to grow in well-drained garden soil, not too dry. It tends to spread. For cut flowers, the first flower should be fully grown. Propagate by dividing the plant.

Physostegia virginiana "Snow Spire"

Platycodon grandiflorum "Apoyama", Balloon flower

Platycodon

Balloon flower

○ ↕ 50-70 ○ ◐ ❁ 7-8 ✂

The name *Platycodon* is composed from the Greek words "platos" (broad, flat) and "kodon" (bell), which refers to the shape of the flower. There is only one species, and this is indigenous in eastern and northern Asia.

P. grandiflora has vertical branching stems, bluish-green, oval or lanceolate, irregular, serrated leaves, and large, wide, bell-shaped, lilac-blue, pink or white flowers which look rather like a balloon before they open; "Albus", 40 cm, has white flowers; "Apoyama", 25 cm, is a dwarf variety with violet-blue flowers; "Florist White", "Florist Rose" and "Florist Blue", 60 cm, have large, white, pink or blue flowers; "Mariesii", 40 cm, flowers profusely with pale blue flowers; "Perlmutterschale", 60 cm, is a pearly pink.

This plant requires light, nutritious, well-drained soil. It appears late in the spring, so it is a good idea to mark the place to prevent it from being hoed up. For cut flowers, the buds should not yet be open. Propagate from seed (April/May) for flowers in the following year.

Polemonium

Jacob's ladder

○ ↕ 25-100 ◐ ❁ 5-8

Polemonium is indigenous in North America, Europe and Asia. It self-seeds so profusely that it may become a nuisance; prevent seed formation by removing the parts which have flowered immediately after flowering.

This plant has composite, pinnate leaves, consisting of pairs of leaflets opposite each other, and a terminal leaf, and clusters of blue flowers with white or yellow hearts.

P. caeruleum, 50-90 cm, flowers from May to June. It has broad, bushy clumps of composite leaves with broad, pointed leaflets, sturdy vertical stems which branch out at the top, and have numerous, wide open lilac-blue flowers with a yellow heart and protruding, bright yellow anthers.

P. caeruleum var. *himalayanum* has purplish-blue flowers twice the size.

P. pauciflorum, 40-60 cm, flowers from June to August, with long, trowel-shaped pale yellow or orange flowers. It is not really winter-hardy. *P. reptans*, 30-60 cm, flowers from May to June. It is a creeping plant with blue flowers.
This is an easy plant to grow in nutritious soil which retains moisture. If necessary, cover in winter. Propagate from seed and by dividing the plants.

Polygonatum odoratum var. thunbergii, Solomons's seal

Polygonatum

Solomon's seal

○ ↕ 50-100 ◐ ❁ 5-6 ! ✂

A number of varieties of *Polygonatum*, is indigenous in the northern hemisphere. The dark blue or red berries which appear when the plant has flowered are poisonous, though they are very attractive to birds.
The plant has thick, creeping rootstocks, unbranching, vertical or elegantly curved stems with irregularly spaced, oval or long leaves in rings or pairs, and one or more hanging, white, yellow or green bell-shaped flowers in the leaf axilla.
P. multiflorum, 60-100 cm, has cylindrical stems, long or oval leaves with short stalks and clusters of two to seven white flowers in the leaf axilla. *P. odoratum*, 30-50 cm, has angular, curved stems, silvery leaves at irregular intervals, and one or more hanging white flowers. The white flowers of the variety, *P. thunbergii*, grow on long, elegantly curved stems. *P. verticillatum*, 70-120 cm, has angular stems in rings, narrow leaves and purple flowers which grow singly or in clusters.
This plant thrives in soil which is not too moist and is rich in humus. Add organic manure. Do not cut too many stems from one plant. Propagate by dividing rootstocks. Attracts bumblebees.

Polemonium caeruleum var. himalayanum, Jacob's ladder

Potentilla fruticosa "Sommerflor"

Potentilla

50-150 6-9

Potentilla is found mainly in the temperate zones of the northern hemisphere. It comprises annuals as well as perennial plants and (semi-)shrubs: a number of varieties grow wild in this part of the world. *P. fruticosa* and cultivated varieties are the main shrubs available.
P. fruticosa is a compact shrub which loses its deeply indented leaves and has bright yellow flowers. "Abbotswood", 50-80 cm, flowers from May to October. It has broad, bluish-green leaves and large white flowers with a yellow heart; "Elizabeth", 50 cm, has large yellow flowers; "Goldfinger", 60-80 cm, flowers from June to October. It has bright green leaves and many beautiful yellow flowers; "Klondike", 100 cm, is golden-yellow; "Maannelys", 70 cm, is lemon-yellow; "Sommerflor", 50 cm, is broad and round with bluish-green leaves. It flowers profusely with large, deep yellow flowers. This plant does well in any well-drained soil. Prune back in March to encourage bushy growth and more flowers. Propagate from cuttings.

Pulmonaria

Lungwort

20-40 3-6

The name *Pulmonaria* is derived from the Latin word "pulmo" (lung). It is indigenous in Europe and Asia, and was used in the past as a remedy for lung diseases.
The plant has creeping rootstocks, beautiful, coarse-haired, broad, oval, pointed ground leaves with long stalks, vertical leafy stems and funnel-shaped flowers which turn from red to blue; the leaves can have whitish spots.
P. angustifolia, 20-30 cm, has unspotted, long, lanceolate ground leaves, stalkless leaves on the stems, and flowers which turn from purplish-red to a bright blue.
P. longifolia flowers from May to June. It has narrow leaves and flowers which turn from purplish-red to violet-blue. *P. officinalis*, 30 cm, flowers from March to April. It has

spotted, pale green leaves and the flowers turn from pink to violet-blue. *P. rubra*, 30-40 cm, flowers from March to May, and has broad, unspotted leaves and red flowers. *P. saccharata*, 25 cm, flowers from April to May. It has colourful leaves, and the flowers turn from reddish-purple to violet.
This plant is good for ground cover.
It requires moist soil, rich in humus.
If necessary, lift the clumps every three years, divide and plant out again for compact growth. Propagate by dividing (in spring or autumn).

Pulmonaria rubra, *Lungwort*

Rodgersia aesculifolia

Rodgersia

○ ↕ 80-180 ◐ ● ❁ 6-8

Rodgersia is indigenous in China, Japan and Korea. It has decorative leaves as well as plumes of flowers.
This plant has elegantly shaped composite leaves with long stalks, and large, branching, cream-coloured, white, pink or red plumes of flowers on long stems.
R. aesculifolia, 100-180 cm, flowers from June to July. It has brown, hairy stems and leaves comprised of five to seven serrated leaflets and whitish-pink plumes of flowers.
R. pinnata, 100-120 cm, flowers from July to August. It is slightly smaller with creamy-pink plumes of flowers.
R. podophylla, 80 cm, flowers in June and July. It has very decorative, red, purple and bronze leaves which are green in the shade, with broad leaflets divided into four, and creamy-white plumes of flowers.
This plant requires nutritious soil which retains moisture and is rich in humus.
If necessary, dig in some manure before planting out. Propagate from seed, root cuttings and by dividing plants (spring/autumn).

Rudbeckia

Black-eyed Susan

40-200 35 7-9

Rudbeckia is indigenous in North America. In general, it has yellow flowers with a dark brown, raised heart. The deep pink *Echinacea purpurea* is sometimes mistaken for *R. purpurea. R. fulgida*, 60-100 cm, has slightly hairy, lanceolate ground leaves with long stalks, very leafy stems which branch out at the top, and flowers consisting of orangey-yellow petals with a brownish-black heart. *R. fulgida* var. *speciosa*, 50 cm, flowers profusely from August to October with orangey-yellow flowers; *R. fulgida* var. *sullivantii*, 40-60 cm, flowers from July to October. It has dark yellow flowers with a black heart; "Goldsturm" is a dark saffron yellow with a black heart, *R. laciniata*, 80-250 cm, flowers from July to September, usually with (semi-)composite flowers, yellow petals and a greenish-yellow heart; "Golden Glow", 200 cm, has golden-yellow composite flowers. *R. nitida*, 100-120 cm, flowers from July to September. It has large

Rudbeckia fulgida "Goldsturm", "Golden Glow" and Stachys byzantina, Black-eyed Susan

Salvia nemorosa "Ost Friesland", Sage

flowerheads with yellow, folded back petals and a greenish-yellow heart.
This plant requires ordinary, fertile, rather moist garden soil and a sheltered position. Add some manure in spring. Remove dead flowers. For cut flowers, the heart must be half open. Propagate from seed and by dividing plants.

Salvia

Sage

40-100 5-9

The name *Salvia* literally means "saving" or "curing". It has been used since time immemorial as a remedy, for example, for coughs, and as a culinary herb. The genus is commonly found in almost all the temperate and warm regions of the world. The plant has squarish stems, leaves opposite each other, and tube-shaped, white, pink, red or blue flowers with two lips in clusters or ears.
S. nemorosa, 40-60 cm, flowers from June to September. It is a grey, hairy plant with vertical, violet-red stems, long, lanceolate leaves, and light blue flowering ears; "Ostfriesland", 40 cm, flowers for a long time with violet flowering ears. *S. officinalis*, 60 cm., flowers from May to June. It is a bushy, greyish, fragrant plant with long, lanceolate, slightly serrated leaves, and pale violet flowers which stand in rings in long flowering ears; "Icterina" has variegated yellow leaves; "Tricolor" has bluish-green, yellowish-white spotted leaves which turn a pinky red.
This plant thrives in any fertile, well-drained garden soil. Lift the plant every three or four years, divide and plant again. *S. officinalis* should be regularly pruned to prevent it from becoming bare. Propagate by dividing the plant. Attracts bees.

Scabiosa

Scabious

40-90 7-10

The name *Scabiosa* is derived from the disease, scabies, and was used in the past as a remedy against it, though the species which has this property is now called *Knautia*. The genus is mainly indigenous in Mediterranean regions. The plant has slender stems, leaves which grow opposite each other, and flat or spherical flowerheads.
S. caucasica, 60-90 cm, flowers from June to September. The stems do not branch out much, and have beautiful, elegant, blue flowerheads with a paler heart. It is good for cut flowers; "Clive Greaves" has lavender flowers; "Fama" has dark blue flowers; "Miss Willmott" has soft white flowers; "Stäfa" has deep blue flowers.
S. japonica, 20 cm, flowers from June to August. It has branching stems, small, pale lilac flowerheads, and is an easy plant to grow in any reasonably nutritious, lime-rich, well-drained soil which is not too wet. Grow in a sheltered spot and support if necessary. Divide every two years. Remove dead flowers. For cut flowers, the flowers should be half open. Propagate by dividing plants.

Scabiosa caucasica "Clive Greaves", Scabious

Sedum kamtschaticum "Variegatum", Stonecrop

Sedum spectabile "Brilliant", Stonecrop

Sedum

Stonecrop

15-60 15-20 6-9

The name *Sedum* is derived from the Latin word "sedere" (to sit), which refers to the way in which some species grow on rocks and walls. It is indigenous in the northern hemisphere and comprises annuals, biennials and perennials.

This plant has a low, compact growth, fleshy, overlapping, often hairy leaves which may have a waxy layer, and small flowers in groups or umbels.

S. acre, 15 cm, flowers in June and July. It forms clumps, stays green and has yellowish-green, irregularly distributed, oval or triangular leaves and bright yellow flowers. *S. aizoon*, 30-60 cm, flowers from June to July. It loses its leaves. It has bright green, lanceolate, serrated leaves and yellowish-orange small clusters of flowers. *A. album*, 20 cm, June to July, is a winter-hardy plant which forms clumps. It has creeping stems, fleshy long, oval leaves which are rounded at the bottom, and numerous white flowers; "Murale" has pale pink flowers and reddish-brown stems and leaves. *S. ewersii*, 20-25 cm, flowers in July and August. It is winter-hardy, has horizontal, branching stems, fleshy, oval, bluish-green leaves, slightly pink on the edges, and purplish-pink compact clusters of flowers. *S. floriferum*, 15 cm, is a bushy evergreen plant which forms clumps with dark green, slightly serrated, spatulate or lanceolate leaves and bright yellow flowers; "Weihenstephaner Gold" has golden-yellow flowers. *S. kamtschaticum*, 20-25 cm, flowers from June to September. It is hardy in winter, has rather limp stems, shiny, dark green, inverted, oval, serrated leaves, and numerous orangey-yellow flowers: "Variegatum" has green leaves with a cream edge. *S. spectabile*, 30-50 cm, flowers from August to September. It is hardy in winter and has erect stems with groups of large, bluish-grey, oval serrated leaves, and countless pinky-red compact clusters of flowers; "Brilliant" has light or bright-red, compact flat clusters of flowers; "Herbstfreude" has orangey-red umbels. *S. telephium*, 20-40 cm, flowers from July to August. It is hardy in winter, has erect stems, long, oval serrated leaves, and hemispherical purplish-red clusters of flowers. It is also suitable for rockeries and walls, and thrives in dry soil in a sunny spot. Propagate from cuttings or by dividing plants. *S. spectabile* is one of the species which attracts butterflies.

Sempervivum tectorum "Smaragd", Houseleek

Sempervivum

Houseleek

5-10 6-8

Sempervivum is indigenous in southern Europe, where it is planted on roofs and walls as a lightning conductor. There are countless hybrids and varieties, and enthusiasts can even become members of a Sempervivum society.

This plant has large rosettes with virtually no stems, and smaller rosettes which develop from runners. The vertical flower stems grow from the heart and usually have several red flowers which die off after flowering.

S. arachnoideum flowers from July to August. There are silvery-white fibrous threads between the tops of the leaves, small rosettes of long, bright green leaves flattened at the top, and stems with bright crimson flowers, closely grouped in clusters of three to seven. *S. tectorum* flowers from June to August. It has large rosettes, many secondary rosettes, dark green, inverted, oval, hairy, fimbriate leaves with brownish-red pointed tips and star-shaped, compact, pink clusters of flowers; "Smaragd" has more compact rosettes. *S. zelebori* flowers in July, and has small, greyish-green spherical rosettes. The stems have about ten greenish-yellow flowers; "Triste" has coppery rosettes and dark pink flowers.

This is an easy plant which has few requirements. The soil should not be too wet. Place in a sunny spot. Propagate by dividing plants and from runners.

Solidago "Dzintra", Goldenrod

Sidalcea

Greek Mallow

50-80 6-8

Sidalcea is a decorative plant from North America with leaves with stalks which are often lobed or pinnate, and ear-shaped and white, pink or purple clusters of flowers. The regular flowers have five petals.
S. candida, 100 cm, proliferates everywhere. It has limp stems and white flowers; "Bianca" has white flowers and sturdier stems. *S. malviflora*, 60-100 cm, has hairy, erect stems, long kidney-shaped, serrated leaves with stalks, the top one with five leaflets, and unbranched pink or purple flowering ears. *Sidalcea* hybrids, 80 cm, have leafy stems, e.g., "Brilliant", which has bright, brilliant red flowers; "Elsie Hugh" has light pink flowers; "Mr. Lindberg" has peony-red flowers; "Sussex Beauty" has pinky-red flowers.
This plant thrives in any sandy, not too dry soil. Remove stems as soon as flowers have wilted to encourage second flowering; for cut flowers, the first flower must be open. Propagate from seed and by dividing the plants (spring/autumn).

Sidalcea "Elsie Heugh", Greek Mallow

Solidago

Goldenrod

60-40 7-9

The name *Solidago* is composed from the Latin words "solidus" (sturdy) and "agere" (to make). In the past it was believed to have medicinal properties. Most varieties are indigenous in North and South America; in Europe, mainly hybrids are available. This plant has straight stems, single leaves and usually yellow flowers in clusters, ears or umbels.
Solidago hybrids, 60-140 cm, have slightly hairy, lanceolate leaves, serrated towards the tip, and small yellow flowerheads in large, broad, slightly curved, pyramid-shaped plumes, e.g., "Dzintra" has deep yellow, star-shaped clusters of flowers; "Golden Mosa", 60 cm, flowers from August to

October, with deep yellow, branching, pointed plumes of flowers; "Lemon Queen" has whitish-yellow flowers with a yellow heart; "Lemore", 60-90 cm, flowers from August to September, with compact, slightly spherical plumes of flowers; "Leraft" flowers from July to August, with dark yellow, slightly pendent, pyramid-shaped plumes; "Praecox", 50 cm, flowers in June and July. It has an erect inflorescence of yellow flowers with an orangey-yellow heart; "Strahlenkrone", 40-60 cm, flowers from July to September, with golden-yellow, star-shaped clusters of flowers.
This plant is easy to grow in ordinary, not too dry garden soil. Occasionally lift clumps and add manure to the soil. For cut flowers, the flowers must be half open. Propagate by dividing the plants (outer parts of clump).

Stachys

Lamb's tongue

30-70 6-8

Stachys is indigenous in temperate and subtropical regions. A number are also indigenous in Europe, such as the unpleasant smelling *S. sylvatica*. The tasty bulbs of *S. affinis* are known as "krosne" or Japanese potato.
This plant has slightly wrinkled, serrated leaves opposite each other. Sometimes there are lower leaf rosettes and leafy, flowering ears.
S. byzantina (syn. *S. lanata*, *S. olympica*), 30-45 cm, flowers in July and August. It has attractive, felt-like rosettes of woolly, hairy, pale greyish-green, long, oval leaves and lilac-pink flowering ears, and is good for ground cover; "Cotton Ball" has large rosettes of big, grey, felt-like leaves and small, felt-like cotton balls instead of flowers; "Silver Carpet" has compact, silvery-grey rosettes and does not flower.
S. menthifolia (syn. *S. grandiflora*, *S. macrantha*), 30-60 cm, flowers in July and August. It forms clumps and has fairly broad, round, serrated leaves and erect, lilac-pink flowering ears with flowers in rings; "Alba" has white flowers.
This plant requires nutritious, well-drained soil. *S. byzantina* can also be planted in drier soil. Plants can be lifted every three years, divided and planted out again.
Propagate by dividing plant (spring/autumn) and from seed.

Stachys byzantina, Lamb's tongue

Thalictrum aquilegifolium hybrids, Meadow rue

Thalictrum

Meadow rue

50-150 30 5-8

Thalictrum is indigenous in the northern hemisphere, South America, and tropical and southern Africa. *T. flavum* and *T. minus* are also found in this part of the world. This plant has parted leaves at the base, stems with few leaves and clusters or plumes of small flowers at the top with so many stamens that they can resemble a pincushion.
T. aquilegifolium, 40-90 cm, flowers from May to July. It has bluish-green parted leaves, lobed, serrated leaflets, light clusters full of purple flowers, with yellow or purple anthers; "Thundercloud" has dark purple flowers. *T. delavayi*, Chinese rue, 200 cm, flowers from June to August. It has parted leaves, serrated or smooth-edged leaflets and long, narrow, pyramidical clusters of fairly large, nodding, lilac flowers with yellow anthers; "Album" has white flowers; "Hewitt's Double" has composite, mauve flowers and makes good cut flowers. *T. rochebrunianum*, 120 cm, flowers from June to August, and has large branching plumes of pinkish-blue flowers with yellow stamens. This plant requires nutritious, well-drained soil, not too dry. Taller species need support. Propagate from seed and by dividing plant. Attracts bees.

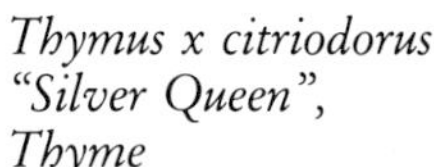

Thymus x citriodorus "Silver Queen", Thyme

Thymus

Thyme

5-25 6-8

Thymus is indigenous in Europe, Asia and Africa. It is a well-known culinary herb and is used as a remedy for coughs. It is a fragrant creeping or standing shrub with thin twigs, oval, round or long leaves, and pink or purplish-red and white flowers in rings.
T. x citriodorus, lemon thyme, 10-20 cm, flowers in July and August. It has a strong lemony smell. It is a compact shrub with erect, hairy stems, shiny green, oval, lanceolate leaves on short stalks, and pale pink flowers; "Silver Posie" has pale green

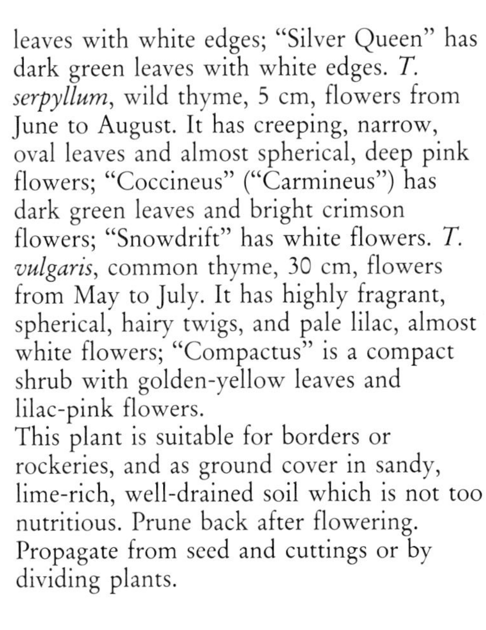

leaves with white edges; "Silver Queen" has dark green leaves with white edges. *T. serpyllum*, wild thyme, 5 cm, flowers from June to August. It has creeping, narrow, oval leaves and almost spherical, deep pink flowers; "Coccineus" ("Carmineus") has dark green leaves and bright crimson flowers; "Snowdrift" has white flowers. *T. vulgaris*, common thyme, 30 cm, flowers from May to July. It has highly fragrant, spherical, hairy twigs, and pale lilac, almost white flowers; "Compactus" is a compact shrub with golden-yellow leaves and lilac-pink flowers.
This plant is suitable for borders or rockeries, and as ground cover in sandy, lime-rich, well-drained soil which is not too nutritious. Prune back after flowering. Propagate from seed and cuttings or by dividing plants.

Verbena

30-150 20 7-10

Verbena is mainly indigenous in the tropical and subtropical regions of America; there are only a few varieties in Europe, including *V. officinalis*, which grows in this part of the world.
This plant is often covered with coarse hair. It has pairs or rings of serrated leaves and flowers growing in ears or umbels.
V. bonariensis, 80-150 cm. The hairy stems have few leaves and do not branch out much. It has lilac flowering ears in groups.
V. hastata, 150 cm, has branching, leafy stems, and compact, lavender-blue or purple plumes of flowers; "Alba" has white flowers; "Rosea" has pink flowers. *Verbena* hybrids are annuals and are divided into fairly tall varieties (30-40 cm), such as "Trophic", which has large, cherry-red clusters, and dwarf varieties (20 cm), such as "Sparkle Mixed", which sprawls and is brightly coloured.
The plants are not winter-hardy and are therefore treated as annuals or biennials, although *V. bonariensis* can last for two seasons. The plant thrives in normal, manured garden soil. Propagate from seed and from cuttings.

Verbena bonariensis

Veronicastrum virginicum "Album"

Veronicastrum

60-200 7-9

Veronicastrum is indigenous in the humid areas of North America. It is closely related to the genus, *Veronica*.
V. virginicum (syn. *Veronica virginica*) has erect, slightly hairy stems, lanceolate, finely serrated leaves on short stalks arranged in rings, and pale blue flowers in large numbers of straight, branching, ear-shaped clusters. In the top axilla the stamens protrude far outside the flowers; "Album" has white flowers, sometimes with a pinkish tinge; "Rosea" has pink flowers.
This plant requires moist, nutritious soil which is not too light. For cut flowers, half of the flowers of the cluster must be open. Propagate from seed and by dividing the plant.

Viola

Violet

15-40 4-7

Viola is found all over the world, but mainly in temperate regions and tropical mountain areas. It comprises annuals biennials and perennials. Depending on the variety, violets can have a beautiful fragrance. The plant usually has spreading, single leaves with small supporting leaves, single flowers in the leaf axilla with five petals. The shape of the flower can only be divided into two equal halves in one way - the lower petal is larger, forming a spur which contains nectar. *V. cornuta*, horned violet, 15-25 cm, flowers from May to July. It has branching stems, heart-shaped, serrated, pointed leaves, coarsely serrated supporting leaves, fragrant lilac or purple flowers with a small yellow eye, on long stems; "Alba" and "Cornetto" have white flowers; "Bullion" has bright yellow flowers; "Old Copper" has coppery-yellow flowers. *V. odorata*, the March violet, has stalkless, round, heart-shaped serrated leaves, narrow, smooth-edged supporting leaves, and highly fragrant, purple, violet, pink or white flowers; "The Czar" has violet-blue, fragrant flowers. There are many hybrids, including "Amethyst", which is a beautiful blue; "Anneke", which is a reddish violet; "John Wallmark", which is lilac, and "Purple Bedder", which is a deep purple. This plant requires cool, moist soil, not too wet in winter, possibly adding some clay or loam. Cover lightly in winter, take up clumps occasionally, add manure and plant out again. For cut flowers, the flowers should be almost open. Propagate by dividing the plant and from cuttings.

Waldsteinia

15-25 4-5

Waldsteinia is indigenous in the northern hemisphere. The shape is similar to that of a strawberry, but the dry, hairy fruit is not edible.
This plant is used as ground cover, and has rosettes of composite or lobed leaves with long stalks, golden-yellow flowers with five, broad, round petals, and numerous stamens in the heart.
W. ternata forms clumps. It is an evergreen

Viola cornuta
"Old Copper", Violet

plant with dark green, shiny, serrated leaves indented in three places, with yellow clusters of two or three flowers. It can spread in a short time with its fast-growing runners to form a thick carpet of ground cover.

This plant thrives in any good garden soil, rich in humus. If necessary, remove runners to prevent plant proliferating. Propagate by dividing the plant.

Waldsteinia ternata

Summary

To design the border, the important factors are the time of flowering, the colour and the height. The table below is intended as a guide; the information given is of a general nature; for the many colour combinations and specific varieties, consult the description.

Height of plant, flowering period and colours of flowers

plant	height in cm	flowering period	colours
Helleborus	30-80	Dec.-April	yellow, green, red, pink, white
Pulmonaria	20-40	March-June	blue, red, violet
Omphalodes	15-20	April-May	blue, white
Waldsteinia	15-25	April-May	yellow
Bergenia	30-50	April-May	lilac, red, pink, white
Brunnera	40-60	April-May	blue
Arabis	10-30	April-June	lilac, pink, white
Dicentra	20-80	April-June	red, pink, white
Viola	15-40	April-July	blue, yellow, red, pink, purple, violet, white
Doronicum	30-80	April-July	yellow
Anchusa	60-150	April-Aug.	blue, purple
Fragaria	10-20	May-June	white
Ajuga	15-25	May-June	blue, purple, pink, white
Iberis	20-30	May-June	purple, red, pink, white
Lunaria	30-100	May-June	lilac, purple, pink, white
Aquilegia	40-80	May-June	blue, yellow, purple, red, violet, white
Incarvillea	50-60	May-June	purple, pink
Polygonatum	50-100	May-June	yellow, green, purple, white
Euphorbia	15-80	May-July	yellow, green, orange, red, white
Aster	15-250	May-July	blue, purple, red, pink, violet, white
Hesperis	60-100	May-July	purple, white
Iris	60-125	May-July	blue, yellow, orange, purple, red, pink, violet, white
Geranium	20-90	May-Aug.	blue, lilac, purple, red, pink
Polemonium	25-100	May-Aug.	blue, yellow
Alchemilla	30-50	May-Aug.	yellow
Leucanthemum	50-100	May-Aug.	blue, white
Thalictrum	50-150	May-Aug.	lilac, pink, purple
Dicentra	20-80	May-Sept.	red, pink, white
Phlox	30-120	May-Sept.	blue, orange, purple, red, pink, violet, white
Salvia	40-100	May-Sept.	blue, purple, red, pink, violet, white
Knautia	50-100	May-Sept.	blue, lilac
Meconopsis	30-120	May-Oct.	blue, yellow
Crambe	75-250	June-July	white
Aruncus	150-200	June-July	white
Sempervivum	5-10	June-Aug.	red, pink
Thymus	5-25	June-Aug.	purple, red, pink, white
Linum	20-100	June-Aug.	blue, yellow, red, white

Plants for a sunny spot

Acanthus	Echinacea	Malva
Achillea	Echinops	Meconopsis
Ajuga	Eupatorium	Mimulus
Alcea	Euphorbia	Nepeta
Anaphalis	Filipendula	Nicotiana
Anchusa	Fragaria	Origanum
Aquilegia	Geranium	Perovskia
Arabis	Hesperis	Phlox
Artemisia	Heuchera	Physostegia
Aster	Iberis	Platycodon
Astilbe	Incarvillea	Potentilla
Astrantia	Iris	Rudbeckia
Buphthalmum	Knautia	Salvia
Calamintha	Lavandula	Scabiosa
Campanula	Lavatera	Sedum
Centaurea	Leucanthemum	Sempervivum
Ceratostigma	Liatris	Thalictrum
Chelone	Ligularia	Thymus
Cimicifuga	Linum	Verbena
Coreopsis	Lobelia	Veronicastrum
Crambe	Lunaria	Viola
Delphinium	Lychnis	
Diascia	Lysimachia	

Plants for semi-shade

Aconitum	Fragaria	Platycodon
Actaea	Fuchsia	Polemonium
Ajuga	Geranium	Polygonatum
Alchemilla	Helleborus	Potentilla
Aquilegia	Hemerocallis	Pulmonaria
Aruncus	Hesperis	Rodgersia
Astilbe	Hosta	Rudbeckia
Astrantia	Iris	Salvia
Bergenia	Kirengeshoma	Scabiosa
Brunnera	Ligularia	Sedum
Buphthalmum	Lobelia	Sempervivum
Campanula	Lunaria	Sidalcea
Cimicifuga	Lychnis	Solidago
Dicentra	Meconopsis	Stachys
Digitalis	Mimulus	Thalictrum
Doronicum	Monarda	Veronicastrum
Echinacea	Omphalodes	Viola
Euphorbia	Phlox	Waldsteinia

Plants for a shady spot

Actaea	Kirengeshoma	Pulmonaria
Bergenia	Ligularia	Rodgersia
Doronicum	Omphalodes	Viola
Hosta	Polemonium	Waldsteinia

Ground-cover

Ajuga	Doronicum	Origanum
Alchemilla	Euphorbia	Phlox
Arabis	Fragaria	Pulmonaria
Astilbe	Geranium	Sedum
Bergenia	Hosta	Stachys
Brunnera	Iberis	Thymus
Campanula	Lysimachia	Waldsteinia
Ceratostigma	Nepeta	
Dicentra	Omphalodes	

Evergreen plants

Arabis	Sedum
Bergenia	Sempervivum
Helleborus	Waldsteinia
Iberis	

Plants with decorative leaves

Alchemilla	Hosta
Anaphalis	Salvia
Dicentra	Stachys
Euphorbia	Thymus

Height of plant, flowering period and colours of flowers

plant	height in cm	flowering period	colours
Heuchera	30-60	June-Aug.	red, pink, white
Stachys	30-70	June-Aug.	lilac, purple, pink, white
Nepeta	30-100	June-Aug.	blue, lilac, pink, violet
Lychnis	30-100	June-Aug.	red, pink, white
Campanula	30-150	June-Aug.	blue, pink, violet, white
Buphthalmum	40-60	June-Aug.	yellow
Astilbe	40-120	June-Aug.	lilac, purple, red, pink, white
Astrantia	50-70	June-Aug.	pink
Sidalcea	50-80	June-Aug.	purple, red, pink, white
Digitalis	50-200	June-Aug.	yellow, purple, red, pink, white
Hemerocallis	60-100	June-Aug.	brown, yellow, orange, red, pink
Delphinium	60-180	June-Aug.	blue, purple, pink, violet, white
Rodgersia	80-180	June-Aug.	cream, red, pink, white
Filipendula	100-200	June-Aug.	yellow, red, pink, white
Lysimachia	5-90	June-Sept.	yellow, white
Diascia	10-30	June-Sept.	pink
Sedum	15-60	June-Sept.	yellow, orange, red, pink, white
Mimulus	20-30	June-Sept.	yellow, spotted red
Malva	30-120	June-Sept.	red, pink, violet, white
Origanum	40-60	June-Sept.	lilac, pink, white
Nicotiana	40-100	June-Sept.	yellow, red, violet, white
Coreopsis	40-100	June-Sept.	yellow
Potentilla	50-150	June-Sept.	yellow, red, pink, white
Ligularia	80-150	June-Sept.	yellow, orange
Anaphalis	20-30	July-Aug.	white
Hosta	30-60	July-Aug.	purple, violet, white
Lavandula	30-60	July-Aug.	blue, lilac, red, pink, violet, white
Actaea	30-80	July-Aug.	red, white, black
Centaurea	30-90	July-Aug.	blue, yellow, purple, red, white
Lobelia	50-100	July-Aug.	blue, purple, red, violet, white
Platycodon	50-70	July-Aug.	blue, lilac, pink, white
Acanthus	80-100	July-Aug.	pink, purple, white
Artemisia	15-180	July-Sept.	yellow, white
Achillea	30-60	July-Sept.	yellow, red, pink, white
Rudbeckia	40-200	July-Sept.	yellow, orange
Liatris	50-150	July-Sept.	purple, red, pink, white
Aconitum	50-150	July-Sept.	blue, yellow, purple, violet
Physostegia	60-120	July-Sept.	red, pink, white
Solidago	60-140	July-Sept.	yellow
Veronicastrum	60-200	July-Sept.	blue, pink, violet, white
Echinacea	75-150	July-Sept.	purple, red, white
Monarda	80-120	July-Sept.	lilac, purple, red, pink, white
Chelone	80-120	July-Sept.	pink, white
Echinops	80-150	July-Sept.	blue
Eupatorium	150-300	July-Sept.	purple, red, pink
Alcea	150-300	July-Sept.	yellow, purple, red, pink, white
Verbena	30-150	July-Oct.	blue, lilac, purple, red, pink, violet, white
Scabiosa	40-90	July-Oct.	blue, violet, white
Lavatera	80-200	July-Oct.	pink
Fuchsia	100-150	July-Oct.	blue, orange, purple, red, pink, white
Calamintha	20-80	Aug.-Sept.	lilac, pink, white
Kirengeshoma	75-90	Aug.-Sept.	yellow
Perovskia	100-150	Aug.-Sept.	purplish-blue
Aster	15-250	Aug.-Nov.	blue, yellow, purple, red, pink, violet, white
Cimicifuga	80-200	Aug.-Nov.	white
Ceratostigma	20-30	Sept.-Oct.	blue

Planting and maintenance

The right soil and correct amount of fertilizers and moisture as well as planting distances determine the result. The choice of varieties in the border is in principle best adjusted to suit the position of the various types of soil of the garden, so that artificial treatment is unnecessary. Building materials, such as wood and stone (flagstone path) can create variety. These days, most plants are cultivated in pots and can be planted at any time of the year, apart from during frost and extreme dry spells. It is preferable, however, to choose the plant's dormant period for planting: spring flowering plants during the autumn and later flowering species during the spring.
Pay particular attention to the amount of shade in the garden: plant descriptions normally tell you whether they prefer sun or (partial) shade. Find out what the sun does in your garden - full sun means 7 - 8 hours during fine weather and partial shade means 4 - 6 hours, but even plants for shade (meaning less than 3 hours) need light.
Sometimes 'new' gardens are supplied with good quality soil, but usually the necessary groundwork has to be carried out.
Poorer quality soil can, as a rule, be improved: dry, sandy soil retains moisture more easily when organic material (compost or peat) is worked in. Compost also provides extra nutrients. Soil which is difficult to handle, such as clay, becomes lighter when sand is added; but here too, compost and peat help to improve the structure.
Fallow land will usually have to be turned over: simple digging is often enough. Depending on the size of the terrain, single digging is often the simplest.

Maintenance

Perennials frequently stay in the same position for 3 - 5 years. From time to time they will need to be fertilized, with for example spent farmyard manure (approx. half to one wheelbarrow per 10 m^2). The most effective time to do this is during the winter. Compost is also a good fertilizer (one wheelbarrow per 100 m^2).
When planting the border, make a selection according to height: small plants at the front, medium sized ones in the middle, and tall ones at the back, and adjust the planting distances accordingly: small plants should be closer together than big ones.
Even if the plants are positioned in the right place, some work will have to be carried out from time to time, eg. tying up, dead-heading and spreading compost.
Watering should be restricted to just after planting and, if necessary, during prolonged dry spells. If the soil is naturally dry it is best to choose species which are best suited to such conditions. Nature will take care of the rest.
Tall-growing plants will need some support, especially in windy spots. Do not tie the plants to one large stick, which looks unnatural, but place a few tonkin canes around the plants and stretch several layers of string or raffia around them. You can also use brushwood - pruned twigs or branches from larger shrubs or trees.
Regularly removing dead flowerheads means in the case of several varieties that they will flower longer or for the second time, because no energy is expended on setting seed (Viola). Sometimes new flowers are produced when the stems are removed after flowering, eg. in the case of Larkspur (Delphinium). Remember that some plants bear attractive fruit after flowering or have ornamental value during the winter, such as the heads of the Yarrow (Achillea), and the seed pots of the Day lily (Memerocallis) or the Iris.
You should not have a big clear-out during the autumn, so do not cut back stems randomly or sprinkle peat dust everywhere. Leave the stems and the leaves that have come off trees and shrubs where they are, and sprinkle compost on top of that. It looks much more natural and protects the plants against frost.
After 3 - 5 years a perennial border will need to be renewed. Dig up the plants during the spring, divide them and replant the youngest shoots (on the outside) in a free space in the soil, which has been turned over and fertilized. Only early flowering species, such as Lungwort (Pulmonaria) should be divided during the autumn.
All kinds of animals can damage plants, as can diseases. More often than not, the damage disappears of its own accord and no extra action needs to be taken. Spraying is often only temporarily effective and it is expensive. Make sure the plants get the right amount of moisture and light and, if necessary, try a different variety which is less sensitive.
Plants with rust (eg. Hollyhock) should be thrown out.
Perennials can usually be sown out of doors, especially in April and May; a month earlier in a cold-frame. Seeds are available for sale, but you can also obtain them from your own garden (or swop with others). Make sure the seeds stay nice and dry, and store them in a cool place.

Improving the soil
There are two reasons for digging over the soil:
- to improve the structure of the soil and its air and water absorption.
- to make it more fertile by adding humus such as compost, leafmould and farmyard manure.
You may want to leave heavy gardening work to an expert. If you prefer to do it yourself, divide the border into strips two to three metres wide, and dig successive parallel trenches to a spade's depth (about 30 cm). Put the soil from the first trench to one side; then use the soil from the second trench to fill the first, the soil from the third to fill the second, and so on. Finally, use the soil from the first trench to fill the last one. Add humus to each trench after you have dug it. Do not dig trenches which are too wide, as the final effect is not very attractive.

Maintenance

Timetable including the most common types of action; * = applies in general.

	March	April	May	Summer	September	October	November
divide, replant	*	*			Lychnis	Mimulus Pulmonaria	*
sprinkle compost	*	*	*			*	*
manure	Chelone Filipendula Fuchsia Malva Phlox Rudbeckia						Chelone
sowing perennials biennials annuals	(*) (*)	* Lunaria *	* *	Lychnis	Aquilegia *	 *	
taking cuttings	Buxus Delphinium Kirengeshoma		Campanula		Buphthalmum Echinacea Hesperis Iberis Monarda Rudbeckia Scabiosa Sidalcea	Lavatera	
remove dead sections			*	*	*		
support				if necessary			
prune	Potentilla Perovskia		Helenium	after flowering: Iberis Lavandula Nepata	Aconitum	*	
clip into shape	Buxus			Buxus			
cover during winter						Anchusa Astilbe Cerastostigma Fuchsia Helenium Heuchera Iberis Incarvillea Lavatera Mimulus Perovskia Polemonium	

N.B. do not move: Cimifuga, Dicentra, Helleborus.
Protect against frost during winter: Incarvillea, Lobelia fulgens, Verbena.

Honeybee, Apis mellifera

Small fox,
Aglais noticae

Common hover fly, Syrphus ribesli

Scale insect, Aphis fabae

Ladybird, Coccinella punctata

Wren,
Troglodytes troglodytes

Small workers in the garden

Life in the border

A border garden is often a flower garden, full of colours and fragrances. This is how flowers attract attention, not particularly from people, but from insects. The beautiful petals and striking fragrances are very tempting and serve as an advertisement: "Come and get your honey-sweet nectar here !" All this serves just one purpose: reproduction. Seed is necessary to produce the next generation, and there are male and female forms even in the plant world. However the problem is that plants cannot get together. Often insects serve as intermediaries; they act as couriers from the male stamens to the female pistils. They are rewarded with nectar for transporting this pollen. The colours and smells show them the way to the source.

Bees are first-class pollinators. These socially developed insects have to feed an enormous generation of larvae in their hives or nests, and this requires a great deal of nectar. The workers consist of only females which are busy in the flowers day after day. While they are working, the pollen becomes stuck to their hairy bodies and is transferred to other flowers. This also applies to bumblebees and hover flies. The latter are wonderful creatures.

Hover flies

Hover flies behave just like bees or wasps. They look the same, and in this guise they try to keep off insect-eating predators. However, they have no sting, and unarmed and entirely defenceless, they do not manage to mislead everyone, despite their deceptive appearance. As humans, we can identify them by the fact that they can hover in the air without moving.
These amiable creatures are very useful; they make short work of scale insects. The eggs are laid in the middle of a colony of scale insects and then the meat-eating larvae which are hatched from the eggs find the table laid. During the fourteen days of the larva stage, every hover fly larva consumes almost a thousand scale insects. They chase them, lift them up, raise them to their mouth and slurp them empty as though they were drinking a glass of wine. It is such a nutritious diet that after two weeks the larva is big and strong enough to hatch out and be reborn as a hover fly. During the second stage of its life it is a vegetarian and feeds on nectar and pollen. Now ladybirds take over the task of eradicating the scale insects and they are very important in the garden as well.

Spiders are not fooled by the appearance of hover flies and many a hover fly comes to a sticky end in a spider's web. But spiders - particularly the fat, juicy ones - are on the menu of birds such as wrens, which peck them out of their webs with great ease. Thus, a nutritional chain begins with flowers.

Bumblebee,
Bombus terrestris

A useful tip

In order to attract useful creatures such as hover flies and their larvae into the garden it is a good idea to plant flowers which attract them such as marigolds, cornflowers, asters and achillea.

List of symbols

- annual
- biennial
- perennial
- bulbous plant
- tuberous plant
- tree
- shrub
- height in cm
- interval between plants in cm
- full sunlight
- semi-shade
- shade
- flowering months
- winter-hardy
- poisonous
- suitable for cut flowers
- berry
- keep moist at all times, compost should not dry out
- keep moderately moist, compost may dry out slightly
- keep fairly dry, only water during growing period
- spray, avoid spraying when plant is flowering